T0367589

MUSINGS

ROBERT LOHMAN

authorHOUSE®

AuthorHouse™
1663 Liberty Drive
Bloomington, IN 47403
www.authorhouse.com
Phone: 1-800-839-8640

Published by AuthorHouse   04/20/2012

ISBN: 978-1-4685-7232-2 (sc)
ISBN: 978-1-4685-7231-5 (e)

Library of Congress Control Number: 2012905416

ACKNOWLEDGMENTS

I wish to thank Sean Detisch for encouraging me to learn to write and for her helpful and astute comments on my work.

I would also like to express my appreciation to Elvi Salazar for reading every word and for contributing many thoughtful ideas and suggestions.

It is surely true that without their support the book would never have been written.

STORIES

LIZ

She gently replaced the telephone in its cradle. She had expected the call. The hard part was over. From now on it would be like shooting fish in a barrel.

When Elizabeth Barclay was sixteen years old, her father made a suggestion:

"Liz, your mother and I think it would be a good idea for you to attend university in the States. You've done extremely well in English schools and you could certainly attend the college of your choice here, but we think it would broaden your outlook of life if you spend your college years outside England. It will also give an edge to your resume when you begin a career. I have a colleague who is a professor at Princeton and he feels that with your achievements here you would have no trouble being admitted there. What do you think?"

Elizabeth began her first year at Princeton in September of 2004. She was an immediate success. She proved to be an excellent student, became captain of the lacrosse team and was principal oboist in the Princeton University Orchestra. But her main asset was her physical attractiveness. She was blessed with that rare beauty bestowed on some English women like Claire Bloom and Vivian Leigh. The Princeton men were smitten but Elizabeth managed to avoid any serious relationships during the four years she was there while at the same time never wanting for a boyfriend. Her summers were spent in exchange programs in France, Italy and Iran.

She graduated on June 9, 2009 at the top of her class and was chosen to be her Class Valedictorian.

When she had begun her college career at Princeton, she had intended to return to England after graduation and obtain her law degree at an English law school. But during her senior year at Princeton an astonishing new idea began to germinate in her head. She decided what she really wanted to be was the mistress of a large, beautiful English estate and have servants, an active social and cultural life and lots of money. Although she did not relish the idea of marriage, it was probably the only way to achieve her goal.

A few hours on Google and she had discovered her future husband.

Sir Charles Cavenaugh was 56 years old, had been a member of Parliament, had a net worth reported to be in excess of ninety million pounds and was at present a partner in the prestigious law firm of Schriber, Gittleman, Cavenaugh and Fry.

Sir Charles owned two residences, a nine room apartment in London and a one hundred and sixty acre estate named Maidenhead about fifteen miles outside of London. Maidenhead had been in the Cavenaugh family for about three hundred years. Nobody seemed to know how it had obtained it's rather odd name but when Sir Charles became it's owner he saw no reason to change it so Maidenhead it was.

But the most important fact about Sir Charles to Elizabeth was that he had recently been divorced from his wife of twenty five years, the former Sara Brightman, not *the* Sarah Brightman, although she often was required to make the distinction while she was married to Sir Charles.

The divorce was Sara's idea and when it became final she moved to New York where she built a successful career as a photographer, helped along no doubt by the rather generous thirty million pounds Sir Charles settled on her as part of their separation agreement. For his part, Sir Charles resumed his bachelorhood without any signs of major trauma.

The couple had no children so there would be no pesky heirs to prevent Elizabeth from owning the property sometime in the future.

On the first Monday of October Elizabeth appeared at the London offices of Schriber, Gittleman, Cavenaugh and Fry, breezed by the receptionist in the outer lobby and appeared before a woman sitting outside of Sir Charles' private office-presumably his secretary.

"I would like to see Sir Charles."

"Is he expecting you?"

"No, but he will be happy to see me."

And with that, Elizabeth opened the door to Sir Charles' office, stepped in and closed the door behind her.

Sir Charles looked up from some papers he was reading and wondered who this lovely, brazen creature was. Probably some new mail girl whom he hadn't seen before, although they always knocked even if the mail they were delivering was important.

"My name is Elizabeth Barclay and I believe I can be a major asset to this firm." Elizabeth stated, "And if you will take five minutes to read my resume and fifteen minutes to talk to me, I believe you will agree."

And with that she deposited a single page of paper on his desk and sat down in one of the chairs facing him, demurely crossing her rather remarkable legs as she did so. At this point Sir Charles' secretary stuck her head in the door and said, "Shall I call security?"

Sir Charles was not sure what he should do. His visitor obviously had no manners but she was extremely attractive and he decided to waste a few minutes and then get her off his back. "No, Miss Begley, I'll take care of it myself." Twenty minutes later Sir Charles had come to the conclusion that this nervy girl might, in fact, actually be an asset to the firm.

"I'll have to discuss it with my partners and we'll let you know in a few days."

On Friday the call came.

Elizabeth began her employment at Schriber, Gittleman, Cavenaugh and Fry on the third Monday of October. By the end of November it was obvious to everyone that Sir Charles had made a wise choice indeed. Elizabeth had a knack for analyzing long-neglected problems and devising quick and elegant solutions. True, none of these problems would have brought down the firm but in the aggregate they were detrimental to the efficiency of the organization and her solutions were noted and approved by all.

Her personal relationship with Sir Charles began innocently enough. It was her custom to work Saturdays even though the office was officially closed. On occasion Sir Charles also spent some time working weekends and it was inevitable that sooner or later they would pick the same Saturday. It was just before Christmas and Sir Charles invited her to lunch at his club a few blocks from the firm's offices. He found that she was a delightful luncheon companion. And it didn't hurt at all to see the looks of envy from his fellow club members as they eyed this beautiful creature that their friend seemed to have produced as if by magic.

There followed some dinners for two, evenings devoted to opera, ballet and symphony performances and finally an evening of love making at Sir Charles' London apartment.

By the end of January their relationship could no longer be kept secret and Sir Charles proposed and Elizabeth accepted.

They were married on Saturday, March 27, 2010. A few eyebrows were raised because of the thirty two year age difference and Elizabeth's parents expressed some concern about their daughter's decision to forego a career, but the general consensus was that Sir Charles had accomplished an astounding feat by exchanging the fifty four year old Sara for this beautiful and charming girl.

Following the wedding reception the couple departed for a month-long honeymoon in Italy, France and the United States.

At the time of his wedding Sir Charles owned two automobiles, an ancient Rolls Royce and a Maserati. On Sunday, May 9, 2010 he and Elizabeth were chauffeured from his London apartment to Maidenhead by Mr. James Johnson in the Rolls. Mr. Johnson was thirty four years old and had been in Sir Charles' employ for ten years. When not driving the Rolls, Mr. Johnson served as Sir Charles' valet and also as butler if that service was required. Around two in the afternoon they arrived at Maidenhead and Elizabeth saw her new home for the first time. It was indeed magnificent. As she emerged from the Rolls she was greeted by the other three members of Sir Charles' staff: Mrs. Kendrick, the cook, Miss Sorel, the maid and Mr. Crenshaw, the gardener. Right out of "Upstairs Downstairs" thought Elizabeth.

But there was yet one more surprise. Parked in the circular driveway a few feet from the front entrance was a brand new Jaguar—a wedding present from Sir Charles to his new wife.

Elizabeth assumed her role as Lady Cavenaugh in short order. She redefined the duties of the staff which had become a little too casual during the period when Sir Charles was single. Although she had had no experience in dealing with servants, she quickly established that fine line dividing the Lady of the house from those who served her. For their part, the staff accepted their revised status stoically while at the same time wistfully recalling the year or so when Sir Charles himself was their only responsibility.

A week or so after she had arrived at Maidenhead Elizabeth decided that a staff of four was too small to adequately serve her needs but elected to put off approaching Sir Charles on the issue until she could properly assess how easy he was to manipulate.

The next few months passed almost exactly as Elizabeth imagined they would. Sir Charles moved in the highest strata of English society. The couple was invited to many parties and other events where the elite gathered, talked, listened, drank, ate and enjoyed themselves as only those who realize they have made it to these exalted positions can. Elizabeth met members of Parliament, the Royal Family, the prime minister and the top stars of English cultural life including Mick Jagger, Paul McCartney and *the* Sarah Brightman. Everyone was suitably enamored with her beauty, but more than that, her ability to converse intelligently on almost any subject and her rather sharp sense of humor. On occasion she would lapse into fluent French if her conversationalist happened to be from France.

There was only one slightly dark cloud. Sir Charles was, unfortunately, a passionate but rather clumsy and unimaginative lover. Even at her tender age Elizabeth had a fair amount of experience in love making and her new husband didn't rank very high in comparison to several of her previous lovers. However, ninety five percent ain't bad, she thought, and she would figure out some way to get that last five percent.

Sir Charles had two basic routines for his work days. If he intended to return to Maidenhead after work, he would ride to London with Mr. Johnson in the Rolls and return with him in the evening. If he intended to stay in London for a day or two, he drove himself in the Maserati and spent the night at his apartment.

Elizabeth realized that this second version of Sir Charles' schedule offered her the opportunity to improve her sex life but she hadn't worked out the logistics of how exactly to take advantage of this possibility. Certainly extreme care was required. She didn't want to upset the entire applecart just to get a good lay.

It finally dawned on her that the solution might well be right under her nose. On those days when he was not obligated to drive Sir Charles to London, Mr. Johnson had passed a small amount of time with Lady Cavenaugh going over a number of household matters and she wondered if he might be a candidate to remove that small dark cloud. He was certainly attractive enough. But she had no way of knowing if his amorous skills were any better that Sir Charles' or, if so, whether he could be trusted not to make some stupid blunder and sink the whole boat. Maybe she should simply discuss it with him cold turkey. She finally decided to wait a while until she had more time to get to know him and assess his capabilities objectively.

When Sir Charles acquired Maidenhead he spent several million pounds making modifications to bring it into the twenty first century. The lowest floor was below ground level and contained the kitchen, wine cellar and considerable storage space. On the first floor were a large living room, two dining rooms, one large and one small, the library, a game room, a music room and three half-bath rooms. The second floor consisted of a large bedroom suite for Sir Charles and his wife, five guest bedrooms and seven bath rooms. On the third floor Sir Charles had constructed five suites for the servants, each consisting of two bedrooms connected by a bath. At present, one of these was shared by Mrs. Kendrick and Miss Sorel and one was occupied only by Mr. Johnson. Mr. Crenshaw lived in his own cottage about one hundred feet from the main mansion.

Elizabeth decided that the suite occupied by Mr. Johnson would serve as her love nest but she still had to work out the timing. It turned out to be easier than she had first thought. Every Tuesday evening Miss Sorel left to spend Wednesday with her sister in Chelsea Village, about two miles from Maidenhead. It happened Wednesday was also the day Mrs. Kendrick did the week's food shopping. Sir Charles offered to let Mr. Johnson use the Rolls for these trips but both Mrs. Kendrick and Miss Sorel preferred to employ a less ostentatious taxi whose service was then charged to Sir Charles.

As a result of these arrangements there was a two to three hour window when the only occupants of the main mansion at Maidenhead were Elizabeth and Mr. Johnson.

It took another month or so but finally Mr. Johnson succumbed to the irresistible charms of his mistress and the dark cloud gave way to clear skies. Elizabeth was concerned about how she was going to manage this situation when she added more staff but, for now, she would, Scarlett O'Hara wise, worry about that tomorrow.

Edward Crenshaw had been employed as the grounds keeper at Maidenhead for thirty one years, even before the first Lady Cavenaugh arrived. Edward was very fond of Sara but, of course, he always called her M'Lady when he spoke to her. She was an avid gardener and often donned coveralls very similar to the ones worn by Edward himself when she worked along with him on innumerable landscaping and horticultural projects over the years. She was an excellent photographer and kept a picture record of the achievements she and Edward had accomplished together. She made a copy of this album and gave it to Edward as a gift when she departed Maidenhead for New York. She also gave him an expensive camera and taught him how to use it.

Edward wasn't so sure about this new Lady Cavenaugh-in his opinion a snip who had tricked Sir Charles so that she could one day own Maidenhead outright. But Edward kept these thoughts to himself except for some grousing to his daughter, Kate, who lived in Chelsea Village and whom he saw a couple of times a month.

"Pop, you're seventy one years old. Just stick it out. Sir Charles will figure this out himself and she'll be gone. Or, you'll be dead and buried before she achieves her goal. So enjoy your new camera and forget about her!"

Kate was not known to concern herself with what she considered to be trivial problems.

Elizabeth's secret lovefests continued without a hitch for a couple of months but around October first she decided that they had to stop. She really needed to add more staff and she had grown weary of Mr. Johnson's attentions, although they were more interesting than those of Sir Charles. On Wednesday, October 13 Sir Charles expected to be away until Thursday evening and Elizabeth decided she would inform Mr. Johnson of her decision at their scheduled rendezvous that morning.

Normally Mr. Crenshaw replaced all the freshly cut flowers in the house on Friday, but he decided to do this on Wednesday because Sir Charles and Lady Cavenaugh were planning guests for dinner Thursday evening after Sir Charles returned from London.

As he approached the mansion he noticed the Rolls and Jaguar were both in their places in the garage which meant he would probably encounter her Ladyship either practicing her oboe or playing the piano as had happened several times before when he was replacing flowers. He rarely saw Mr. Johnson who normally confined himself to his third floor bedroom.

But there was no sound to be heard at all when he entered the house and a tiny seed of suspicion began to grow in Mr. Crenshaw's head. He completed his task by photographing a few of the flower arrangements with his new camera. He had done this before and his daughter had emailed them to Sara in New York.

Edward was torn between his natural tendency to not pry into the affairs of others and his increasing desire to find out exactly where her Ladyship was. As he approached the servant's suites on the third floor he noticed that the door of the bedroom assigned to Mr. Johnson was closed but the door to its presently unoccupied twin was open. He entered the room, crouched behind the bed and peered into Mr. Johnson's bedroom through the two open doors of the bathroom. With his suspicions confirmed, he decided to record the activity taking place there by her Ladyship and Mr. Johnson with his camera. He turned off the flash, set the camera to video mode and held it just above the bed and recorded about ten seconds of what appeared to be rather vigorous lovemaking. He was not at all sure why he was doing this but once he was finished he quietly left the third floor and returned to his cottage.

Mr. Johnson took the news that his amorous adventures with her Ladyship were over with equanimity and the party Thursday night went well. Some of the guests commented on the beautiful flower arrangements.

On Sunday Mr. Crenshaw visited his daughter and after considerable trepidation showed her the results of his photographic activity the previous Wednesday.

"Pop, you want to get rid of her, here's your chance." she said. "You want to not rock the boat, just keep the stuff for some possible future use. Leave the camera here. I'll send the flower pictures to Sara but not the rest. When you decide what you want to do, let me know."

Edward Crenshaw was a master groundskeeper but a mediocre hunter. Even so, on occasion he would walk through some of vast woodlands of Maidenhead and, if lucky, would bring the carcass of some small animal he had manage to shoot to Mrs. Kendrick who would do her best to turn it into a tasty dish.

On the Tuesday following his visit to Kate he was on one of these outings when he stepped into a yellow jacket nest. In his panicky efforts to ward off the ensuing attack he inadvertently discharged his shotgun and became the victim of a fatal accident. A troop of girl scouts, themselves on a walk through the woods, heard the sound of the shot, discovered Edward's body and called the Chelsea Village police.

The subsequent investigation determined that no foul play was involved.

Mr. Crenshaw's funeral was held on Monday, October 25. Over one hundred people attended including all the residents of Maidenhead, Kate and her two children, Kate's ex-husband and Sara, who had flown in from New York. Sara and Sir Charles both spoke of their admiration of Mr. Crenshaw both for his horticultural skills and his basic decency. Sir Charles paid all the funeral expenses and transferred three million pounds to Kate's bank, claiming to HM Revenue and Customs Department that it was from an insurance policy he had taken out on Mr. Crenshaw's life many years ago thus allowing Kate to avoid any tax consequences. HM Revenue and Customs Department accepted this claim without comment.

Kate decided that she would move to the United States with her two children and start a new life there, possibly in New York as an assistant to Sara. As she was making plans for the move, she remembered Mr. Crenshaw's camera. She tried to decide what to do with the camera and its damaging photographs. She really had no reason to hate the present Lady Cavenaugh but she felt that Sir Charles might be better off without her; maybe there was a chance for a reconciliation with Sara. They had seemed friendly enough at the funeral.

In the end she decided to let someone else make the decision and simply dropped the camera off at the Chelsea Village police station along with a short note asking them to dispose of it however they wished.

On Saturday, November 6, Sir Charles was in his library reading when Mr. Johnson knocked and entered.

"Sir Charles, there are two men from the Chelsea police department here who wish to talk to you. Something about Mr. Crenshaw's camera."

"Show them in, Mr. Johnson. That's funny, I didn't even know Mr. Crenshaw had a camera." Sir Charles said.

THE ENCOUNTER

Sophia Bizet had arrived in the U.S. during the summer of 1997 from Bosnia. She was in the third year of a PhD program at Columbia where she hoped to obtain a Doctorate in Mathematics. Sophia had had a rather violent coming of age in Bosnia and adjusted to the pace of life in Manhattan with ease.

In order to pay for her education and afford decent living accommodations in Manhattan she needed a job and soon found one at Five Star Escort Services. Because her escort services were required only in the evening, she was free to attend classes at Columbia during the day. The pay was excellent and she soon found that she had to work only three or four nights a week to meet all her financial obligations. Sophia was beautiful, intelligent and spoke four or five languages and she soon became the most popular escort at Five Star, especially with Japanese clients. Except for a few Japanese escorts, she was probably the only escort in Manhattan who could speak Japanese.

Like all the legitimate escort services in Manhattan, Five Star imposed rather strict rules on their clients' behavior when with their escorts. Clients were expected to pick up their dates at a location chosen by the escort, pay for the evening's entertainment, and return their escort to a destination of her choice when the evening's festivities were over. Escorts were then required to call in to report the length of their date and to insure that they were home safely. No sexual favors were allowed and if an escort wanted to develop some kind of more personal relationship with a client it could not be on company time and the escort was responsible for any mishaps that might arise.

During her time in Manhattan Sophia had had a few casual affairs. But not with clients, although she had many opportunities to do so. Sophia's goal was a professorship at a prestigious university and didn't feel any need to get involved in any romance that would interfere with her ability to achieve her goal.

On rare occasions Sophia would invite a client up to her apartment for a drink but she didn't feel the desire to do that one night in February when her client let her out of his rented limo at her apartment building a little after midnight.

She was just about ready to insert her plastic key into the apartment building front door when she felt a hand on her shoulder and a hard object probing her back.

"Just don't make any noise and you'll be fine." The voice was soft but firm.

"Open the door."

Sophia decided that now was not the time to make a fuss. She opened the door and the two of them entered the building's small lobby. The night clerk's duties ended at 11:00 P.M. so there was no one to see them. They approached the elevator, entered it and Sophia pushed the number of her floor. Her abductor had remained behind her during this time and she had yet to see him. Once inside the elevator he removed his hand from her shoulder and the probe that had been pushing on her back and they met face to face for the first time. He was black, perhaps six feet two and looked like he weighed about one hundred and eighty pounds. There was no probe, only his index finger. Most amazing was his outfit, which consisted of a bright orange jump suit.

"Just shut up until we're inside your apartment, and don't get cute." Sophia had yet to utter a word and decided that remaining silent was the best option she had.

Once inside the apartment, he asked, "What do you do for a living, to afford an apartment like this?"

"I'm an FBI agent," Sophia lied,

"What do you do there?"

"I'm an analyst. I present statistical crime data in such a way that my superiors can understand it."

"Do you carry a gun?"

"No, my job doesn't require me to carry a gun."

Sophia realized that this foolishness was probably not going to last much longer. She also became aware of the fact that she was talking to possibly the most handsome man she had ever met.

"Tit for tat," she said. "What do you do? And why are you dressed in that ridiculous outfit?"

"I'm a convicted felon, and this is what you wear when you're a convicted felon on your way to prison upstate."

"What was your crime?"

"Crimes."

"Alright, what were your crimes?"

"You're the FBI analyst. Look up the ten most crimes. I've probably done most of them."

Sophia decided to try and keep him talking. Sooner or later the company will wonder why she hadn't called.

"What was your favorite crime?" she asked.

"Robbing banks."

"Why do you rob banks?"

"Same as Willie Sutton."

"Who's Willie Sutton?"

"You might say he and I were fellow careerists. Poor Willie is dead now."

Sophia realized that there was some sort of joke here, and she wasn't in on it.

"How did you escape from prison?" she asked.

"I didn't escape from prison. I was on a bus being taken up state and I managed to jump out of the bus and hide in your bushes. They stopped the bus and looked for me for a while but there were only two of them and they really weren't muscle so they gave up. There's probably about a hundred SWAT's looking for me now."

"Did you ever kill anybody?"

"I don't know. When you're in a fire fight with the law all you want to do is get the hell away. You can't wait around to see if you hit anybody or not."

At this point he wanted to see more of the apartment. As they entered the bedroom he noticed her cat lying on the bed.

"What's his name?" he asked.

"It's a she and her name is Debra."

He began to open drawers and soon found the bedside stand where she kept her revolver.

It didn't look like a FBI piece. "I thought you said you didn't carry," he said.

"I don't carry. It's my own. I keep it for protection from guys like you."

Jesus, this chick it too much. Cute though. If she's an FBI agent, I'm Jim Brown.

After a while he said, "Listen I got to get out of here but I can't leave until I get some clothes. Tomorrow you're going to buy me some and then I'll be out of your hair."

"How do you know I won't call the law while I'm gone?"

"Because you love your cat."

The phone rang.

"Yes, this is me. Yeah, I'm fine. O.K., goodnight."

Sleeping arrangements were tricky. He took the gun and cat and installed himself on her living room couch.

"Look, I could tie you up but I'll take a chance. Just don't get smart of I'll probably have to shoot you and the cat. O.K.?"

Sophia said, "Wow, you're really a tough guy. I don't want to mess with you. They'll catch you when you leave anyway. Good night." And into the bedroom she went and closed the door.

He knew that she was putting him on but he had to smile. Five million people in New York and I have to pick a wiseass for a hostage.

Early the next morning Sophia emerged from her bedroom. Her visitor was on the couch, the cat on top of him and the gun resting inches away on the coffee table.

"What's your name?" she asked.

"I don't have a name. Felons have numbers," was the curt reply. "Make some coffee."

"I'm your hostage, not your maid," she replied.

"O.K. I'll make the coffee. You get dressed and ready to go to the clothing store. I can't stay here too long. They'll get search warrants and start busting down every door in this building."

Around nine o'clock Sophia found a men's clothing store reasonably nearby in the Yellow Pages and asked for his sizes.

"I don't know my sizes. Just get me a large jacket, a decent size shirt, socks, a tie, and pants with about a thirty-three inch inseam. Also, an overcoat, a hat and size eleven D shoes. They don't have to fit perfectly. Anything will be better than this stupid jump suit."

"How are you going to pay me back for all this stuff, since it's obvious they will catch you and you'll be back in jail?"

"Listen," he said. "Just be thankful that if you behave yourself you'll get out of this with your skin intact. Don't give me any more bull and get going."

Sophia returned about two hours later with her purchases. The outfit had cost her about twelve hundred dollars but she figured he was right-she could be lying in a pool of blood right now.

"I've got to change. So if you're embarrassed look away. I've still got the gun. Don't try being a heroic FBI crime fighter," he said with as much sarcasm as he could muster up given the spot he was in.

When he finished changing, Sophia asked, "How did you learn to speak so well? You don't talk like a thug."

"I've spent fifteen years in prison. If you behave, they let you take courses."

"Why did you start a life in crime in the first place?" she asked.

"It's long story. My first five were for a crime I didn't do. When I got out I figured, what the hell, I might as well go for broke. I couldn't get a decent job anyway. And for a while I did O.K. But sooner or later some fink sells you out or you make a stupid mistake and you land right back in the slammer. After the second time you don't really have any choice. If they catch me this time, I'll probably never get out again."

Of course, Sophia knew this was how the U.S justice system worked. She began to feel a small glimmer of sympathy for him. His story was certainly sad. If, in fact, it was true.

"Listen," Sophia said, "suppose I could get you out of this mess. Would you give up being a criminal?" Sophia had absolutely no idea how she could accomplish this, but for some reason she blurted it out.

He thought a moment. *This girl is not only a wiseass, she's as crazy as a loon.*

"You said you were an FBI agent. You should be trying to figure out how to arrest me. Not behaving like some soul saver in the Salvation Army."

"You know I'm not an FBI agent. But in my real line of work I meet people who are able to solve all kinds of problems, although I admit yours is about as big a mess as I've ever encountered. You interested or not?"

"I suppose your giving me this line because I didn't whack you when I had the chance. But I needed you to get me the clothes. I'm not sure you or anybody else can get me out of this life."

He realized that he had about two seconds to make up his mind. She was nuts but, really, he had nothing to lose. There was no doubt in his mind that if he got out of this apartment they would catch him sooner or later.

"O.K. What's your plan?" he asked.

"I'll have to go out of town for two or three days. Before I leave I'll get some food in for you and take Debra to the kennel. Stay here and don't make any noise. Just hope they don't pick my apartment to break into with a warrant until I get back. If that happens, you're on your own. But please don't mention my name or I'll be in a pot of trouble, me being an FBI agent and all," Sophia instructed trying to inject a little humor into the proceedings.

"I don't know your name."

"It's Sophia Bizet."

"Bizet like the Carmen guy?" he asked.

"That's the one." I'll be damned. He's trying to impress me.

She then put on her coat, took the cat and left.

As good as her word, she returned with groceries, a bottle of Scotch and shaving supplies.

Fifteen minutes later she left again after packing a small traveling bag.

"If you leave before I get back, just Fed Ex me twelve hundred bucks. I'll throw in the Scotch for free."

On her way to the airport Sophia wondered, "What the hell have I got myself into?"

Frank Baldoni was indeed a very tough guy. At the age of sixty three he had survived moving up through the organized crime business in Chicago and was now the head of the family that bore his name. Like many in his chosen profession he was not a simple man. He could be utterly ruthless in his business dealings but he was a loving husband and father, supported a number of charitable and civic organizations in Chicago and was trying to enter the legitimate business world as well as maintaining his central position in the Chicago underworld. Frank's greatest love outside his family was opera. He was a season ticket holder at the Chicago Opera and rarely missed a performance. There were times when he was required to visit New York and on these visits he always enjoyed an opera at the Metropolitan in Lincoln Center. Although true to his wife, he felt most comfortable attending these events with a beautiful woman and for the past three years the woman who accompanied him was Sophia Bizet. Frank was very fond of Sophia. Besides her beauty, he admired her intelligence, sense of humor and her devotion to opera which matched his own.

He made no attempt to hide his primary business from Sophia and she accepted him as she experienced him: an interesting man in many ways and always a gentleman.

Frank was not annoyed but, even so, rather surprised when his secretary announced that there was a young woman by the name of Sophia Bizet who would like to see him. As he tried to figure out what this might mean, he said, "O.K. Show her in."

Sophia related a somewhat edited version of her problem leaving out those parts she believed might upset Frank such as the fact that her visitor was a black convicted felon who had spent fifteen years in prison. Her abductor became simply a friend who needed some help and she was sure Frank could supply that help. She made up the name Charles Hamming and claimed that she could handle the problem of a picture for the passport when she returned to New York.

Frank knew that he was not getting the whole story, but he had learned over the years not to probe into other people's lives unless it affected his business or the person in question was not to be trusted. Neither of these conditions applied in Sophia's case, so he agreed to provide the items she requested.

It was not a difficult task, more like child's play, really.

"O.K. I'll have them for you the day after tomorrow," he promised.

Two days later Sophia was on a plane headed for New York with a passport, driver's license and birth certificate from Cook County Illinois showing that Charles Hamming had been born in Chicago at Presbyterian Hospital on June 15, 1959.

Sophia's plane arrived in New York that afternoon and she returned to her apartment around seven that evening.

The newly christened Charles Hamming was still there looking as handsome as ever. While she was gone he had considered setting out on his own but had decided that there was no advantage to refusing her help and he might as well hear exactly what her plan was. Besides, she could have turned him in now that the cat was gone and she hadn't.

"You miss me?" Sophia asked. "Why didn't you split while you had the opportunity?"

"I didn't want to spoil your chance for a big FBI promotion," he said, trying to show her she wasn't the only one who could spin a joke.

Sophia took his picture, photo-shopped it and attached it to the passport. She then presented him with the three documents. He was impressed. It occurred to him that he had misjudged her and that she was not only a decent chick but that she was well-connected with somebody, even if she was a wiseass.

He took the documents and said simply, "Thanks."

"Now, here's the drill," said Sophia. "At exactly midnight tonight a limo will arrive at my front door and I'll get out and enter my apartment building. Leave the apartment at midnight and as I walk in you walk out and get in the limo. Don't speak to me or the driver. Just follow his instructions. Is that clear?" she concluded.

"Perfectly. But what are we going to do between now and then?"

"Well," said Sophia, "I'll be leaving around ten. Why don't we just have a drink and see what develops?"

"Suits me," was his reply.

The plan went off without a hitch, at least until he got into the limo. Sophia had no way of knowing what happened after that because the last part of the plan was arranged by Mr. Baldoni.

She disposed of the jump suit in her fireplace and assumed that she had heard the last of Mr. Charles Hamming.

Over the next few years she often wondered if she had really done the right thing. Suppose she had allowed a murderer to go free and he had killed or maimed somebody. Some women or kid. But eventually her time was fully occupied with getting her degree and obtaining the job she wanted with a university. She ended up at MIT in Cambridge, got married to Robert Wirth and had two children.

She had completely forgotten about her traumatic abduction until June 15, 2007 when she received a letter in the mail from Costa Rica. The envelope contained a small clipping from a local newspaper proclaiming in Spanish that a local writer, Charles Hamming, who was originally from the U.S., had just had his first novel accepted for publication by W.W. Norton Company. There was also a bank check made out to Sophia Wirth for twelve hundred dollars.

A hand written note on the clipping read, "Thanks for the Scotch."

THE GIFT

In nineteen seventy four when I was fifty years old I purchased tickets to the Princeton home football games. Although my wife and I had lived in Princeton twenty years at that time, we never felt like true Princetonians because neither of us had graduated from Princeton and I suppose I felt that going to all the home football games would increase, however slightly, our feeling that we belonged there.

I had originally hoped to have seats on the Princeton side but found that all the good seats were reserved for Princeton graduates so I settled for two seats on the visitor's side. They were located right on the fifty yard line and gave us a wonderful view of the game.

By nineteen eighty four we had been attending the games for ten years and in early November of that year we were expecting to attend the Cornell game, a game I always enjoyed because of the great Cornell marching band. However, on that particular Saturday, my wife elected to not go to the game because she wanted to listen to "The Marriage Of Figaro" which was being broadcast live from the Met that afternoon.

It was a beautiful crisp day, often referred to as perfect football weather, so I decided to attend the game by myself. We lived about a mile from Palmer Stadium and, as usual, I walked to the stadium from our home. When I arrived at our seats I noticed that one of them was already occupied by a young girl of nineteen or so but I sat down next to her without comment since it was common practice at Palmer Stadium to select a seat at random even if it didn't match your ticket stub and hope that the person assigned to that seat wouldn't show up.

It was hard for me then, at age sixty, to know how to start a conversation with such a young girl but she solved the problem by starting a conversation herself. She was not exactly talkative but friendly in the sort of direct way that young people seem to be nowadays. Without eliciting any information about me at all, she told me she was attending Cornell, was enrolled in the hotel management program there, was twenty years old, was visiting her grandfather here in Princeton who was a Princeton graduate and who was at this moment sitting almost directly across from us on the Princeton side, and finally, that she was sitting next to me because she wanted to root for Cornell and thought it was more appropriate to do so from this side.

After a stirring rendition of the national anthem by the sort of ragamuffin Princeton band (at least when compared to the Cornell band) the game started and it soon became apparent that Terry's (I had finally learned her first name) long suit was not football. Still, it was fun to be sitting next to such a pretty and vibrant young girl and I had resigned myself to spending a pleasant afternoon explaining to her what downs were, why teams usually punted on fourth down etc.

About seven minutes into the game she turned to me and said, "You look sort of sad. Why don't we go to my room at the Inn and I'll try and cheer you up?"

At first I thought I had not heard her correctly and from the look on my face she must have assumed that I didn't understand what she had said. So she continued, "You know, make love, have sex, whatever."

At this I was even more flabbergasted than I had been at her first statement but before I could respond she grabbed my arm and pulled me down our row of seats and out of the stadium. She released my arm but, still in some sort of daze, I followed her like a puppy on a leash as we headed toward Prospect Street and then on to the center of town and the Nassau Inn. It's about a fifteen minute walk from Palmer Stadium to the Nassau Inn and although Terry chattered on in her factual non-editorializing manner the entire way I don't think I uttered one word.

I did plenty of thinking though. What kind of scam is this? Are there thugs waiting to mug me . . . is there a blackmail scheme afoot . . . if she really a pro and just hasn't mentioned price yet?

But I didn't say anything because I was afraid if I did so I would wake up and find myself back at the stadium or that she would disappear in a puff like a witch or genie.

Upon reaching the Inn she marched brazenly in and I followed her right through the main lobby, into the elevator and up to her third floor room without so much as a funny look from anybody as we passed by. Nobody suspects a girl and her grandfather are up to any mischief.

Once in the room conversation more or less stopped and she retired to the bathroom. I didn't know what I was supposed to do but I was sure of one thing: I didn't want her to see my sixty-year old replica of a nude human male so I undressed, climbed into bed and hid under the bed covers so she could see only my face, figuring that she had already absorbed the shock of that.

Shortly she emerged completely nude and looking even more beautiful than when she was fully clothed.

"You don't look quite so sad now," she said as she hopped into bed.

I had never made love to a twenty year old girl before but I went through the motions and did the best I could under the circumstances. She was a proficient rather than a passionate lover and, consistent with her style, neither complimented me nor complained about what I am sure was a rather pale imitation of her former lovers.

Later, as we relaxed, she became more talkative. I learned that she was born in Scarsdale, N.Y., that her mother and father were both lawyers with offices in Manhattan, that she had one brother and one sister, that her childhood was free of stress and that she had played trombone in her high school band. She also explained that she was staying at the Inn during her visit to her grandfather because, as she put it, she preferred having her own space, that her father had gone to Cornell and that I was the eleventh man she had made love with and was by far the oldest. Soon it was three twenty and we both realized we had better head back to the stadium; she to her grandfather and I home.

Our conversation on the way back was perfunctory. I really didn't know what to say without embarrassing myself, her, or both of us but she was the same cheerful non-judgmental person that she had been ever since we first met. I did establish that she had never heard of Raymond Chandler, Harry James, Tyrone Power or Clara Bow. As before, she did not ask me my name or for any other information about me.

When we arrived at the stadium entrance the game was almost over and many people were leaving. She came near me, gave me a slight hug and a peck on the cheek and said one word, "Goodbye."

As she disappeared into the crowd I got such a sinking feeling in the pit of my stomach that I almost passed out.

But then she turned around, approached me and said, "Jesus, you look sadder now than you did before. Get over it! It's seven weeks before Christmas. Just think of it as an early Christmas gift. It was a lot better than a new necktie, wasn't it?"

Ten seconds later she was gone.

I never saw or heard from her again and, of course, I "got over it." But I often think of her. She is forty seven now, probably married with children and maybe even grand children. I wonder how many men she has slept with since that afternoon so long ago and if any of them have broken my record as the oldest.

Today is Saturday and Princeton is playing Cornell at home. I won't be there.

RULES

"Larry, you've got to pay up," said Vince.

"Jesus Christ Vince, I know I've got to pay up. Don't I always pay up? Seven years we been together and I've never not paid up. I know the rules!"

"Larry, we're not together. I'm just the collector for Moss, and I'm here to tell you that you've got to pay by next Tuesday."

"Vince, I just need more time. Didn't you tell him the story?"

"That's how I got you the extension, Larry. One week."

"Jesus, that god damned horse. A seven and a half length lead with an eighth to go and he falls down and breaks his leg. I had the whole deuce on him to win. I would have had six hundred thousand bucks in my hand, six hundred thousand big ones, Vince".

"It's one hell of a story, Larry. But you got to see it from Moss's point of view. He's got a wife and three kids, and a big house and two Mercedes. He lets you get away with this and all the other clients will come up with their own cock and bull tales," said Vince.

"Vince, where the hell am I going to get twenty thousand bucks in one week?" asked Larry.

"Larry, I don't know. Knock off a bank or borrow it from Zelda. I can't solve your problem. I'm just a collector.

If you don't pay by next Tuesday Moss will send a couple of cowboys down here and you'll end up in the hospital for six months. He'll make an example of you so the other clients don't get any wise ideas," added Vince.

"That stupid nag. On top of everything else they had to shoot the poor son of a bitch right there on the god damned track."

"Larry, I got to go. I'll see you here in a week and you better have the money, including the extra vig for the extra week," said Vince. "I don't know. Maybe I'm getting too old for this job. Maybe I should quit and get a job bouncing at some hip club and dig the cute little chicks that come in. Anyway, good luck Larry. I'll see you here in a week."

Larry arrived at his apartment around five that afternoon in a foul mood. He checked the mail-just the usual crap, except for one letter addressed to him by hand in ink. Inside the envelope was a single sheet of paper. When Larry unfolded it something fluttered out and fell to the floor. Larry looked at the piece of paper, saw there was nothing written on either side and reached down and picked up what looked like a check from the floor. It was a check, in fact a cashier's check, from the Chase Manhattan Bank made out to him for the sum of seven million dollars. Larry carefully examined the check. Then he examined it again. It must be a fake or a scam of some kind. He looked at the piece of paper again. Nothing.

Larry sat down and tried to cope with what seemed to be an impossible situation. A check from the Chase Manhattan Bank made out to him for seven million dollars. Jesus, thought Larry, I must be dreaming. How could this happen? Maybe a monumental computer glitch. Larry couldn't figure out what to do. Finally he decided to show it to Zelda. Maybe she would have some ideas. He called her and said he had to see her. Would seven o'clock be okay? Zelda was on another line but put the other party on hold for a second and said, "If you must."

Zelda Chavez was a Cuban immigrant who owned and operated a successful rug cleaning business. She was attractive if not exactly beautiful, knew her way around and tolerated Larry although it was clear that he was not the love of her life.

Zelda would know what to do.

He arrived at Zelda's apartment around seven. She didn't exactly welcome him with great enthusiasm but neither did she look at him as if he were something the cat dragged in-as she sometimes did.

"Hi Zelda, ¿cómo estás?" said Larry. These were the only two Spanish words Larry knew but he often greeted Zelda this way to get her in a good mood.

"Come in Larry," said Zelda trying to suppress a slight smile because she didn't want to give Larry the impression that he could just pop in on her like this any time he was in a jam and needed her to bail him out. Being in some kind of a jam was a normal situation for Larry but Zelda put up with him because he was basically harmless and could be amusing at times.

"What is it this time? Vince on your ass again?"

"Yeah, but that's not why I came. Take a look at this, and tell me what the hell I should do."

Larry passed the envelope with the folded piece of paper and the check to Zelda and then sat down on her sofa and waited.

Zelda carefully looked at all three. She noticed the envelope had no return address.

"Larry, are you trying to drive me nuts. Where the hell did you get this?"

"It came in the mail today," said Larry. "That's all I can tell you. The question is, what should I do with it?"

Zelda sat down on the sofa. After about two minutes, she said, "Larry, the first thing you should do is find out if it's a fake. Take it to the Wells Fargo Bank on Westfield Avenue tomorrow morning and show it to the manager. She can tell you in one second if it's real. If so, use it to open an account there. Then we'll decide what the next step is. Jesus, Larry, maybe you've fallen in a pile of manure and have come out smelling like a rose!"

At nine o'clock Wednesday Larry walked into the lobby of the Wells Fargo Bank. He saw a rather pretty girl with long blond hair sitting in a small office and decided to try his luck with her.

She looked up from whatever she was reading and said, "Good morning, sir. Can I help you?"

Larry was deathly afraid of anybody that had anything to do with banks. But this little girl looked harmless enough.

I'd like to open an account here," said Larry.

"Certainly, sir. Please come in and sit down. All you need to do is to fill out a few forms and make your first deposit and you'll be on your way in no time! Give me a second to get the forms and we'll be off and running."

She left her desk for a moment to retrieve the proper forms from a file cabinet in the corner of her office.

Larry noticed a little triangular wooden block on her desk which held a brass plate which informed him that he had been talking to Sue Ann Welchor.

Sue Ann returned with the forms and Larry carefully filled all of them out. He was doing fine until he came to the line: Initial Deposit Amount. He couldn't put it off any longer. He pushed the check across the desk for Sue Ann to examine.

"Will this do for a start?" he asked.

Sue Ann looked at the check, rose and said, "Mr. King, excuse me for a moment. I'll be right back."

With that she knocked on the door of a larger office and said, "Mr. Hutchins, may I see you a moment?"

She entered the office, the door closed and Larry was left alone to ponder what came next.

Sue Ann returned about ten minutes later.

"Everything is fine Mr. King, and thank you for joining the Wells Fargo family," gushed Sue Ann. "But remember, you must wait five business days before you can draw funds from your account. That would be next Wednesday," she concluded.

Zelda was at work and too busy to talk, but asked him to drop by that evening. He was able to advise her that the bank had accepted the check.

This time Zelda welcomed him with a little more zip than she had last evening.

"Come on in, Larry. I still can't believe it. We've got to figure out how you got this. There must be an angle somewhere."

"I'm still not out of the woods, Zelda. I can't get my hands on any of the money until next Wednesday and I need to pay Vince about twenty five grand on Tuesday."

Zelda pretended that she didn't know what Larry was going to say next. Might as well let him stew for a couple of minutes.

"Zelda, I was thinking maybe you would consider lending me the money so I can pay Vince on Tuesday. I'll pay you back just as soon as I can get the cash out of the bank," said Larry, right on cue.

"Well, let's see. I may be able to do that if you pay me a modest interest, say five grand," said Zelda, having a hard time disguising how much fun it was watching Larry grimace at the mention of the five grand. "O.K.? I'll have it for you tomorrow morning."

"Zelda, you're all heart," said Larry, thinking this broad could teach Moss a thing or two.

The following Tuesday Larry and Vince met at the usual place and time.

"You got it?" asked Vince.

Larry took twenty four brand new thousand dollar bills out of his pocket, and, one by one placed them in Vince's outstretched hand.

"Larry, I'm proud of you," said Vince. "I'm sure Moss will be pleased."

With that, Vince stood up and was gone in ten seconds.

Zelda reexamined the envelope and noticed it was postmarked New York City which didn't help much in trying to figure out who Larry's benefactor was. After a couple of months they quit worrying about the source of the money. This allowed them time to think about what to do with it. Even with the lousy interest paid by Wells Fargo they were getting about fifty eight hundred dollars a month from it, most of which Larry lost at the track.

Larry had never had any money to invest and didn't even know what a stock or a bond was. Zelda, however, was very savvy on how to make money and what to do with it once you had it. Within about three months she had helped Larry open accounts at a number of brokerages and had constructed a well balanced portfolio for him. She also found a competent accountant to handle Larry's tax situation. Larry, of course, had never paid a dollar in taxes, but understood that trying to fool around with the IRS could be worse than dealing with Vince.

As time went along, Zelda decided that life with Larry wouldn't be all that bad and they gradually drifted into a relationship that was remarkably free of stress. They were married about three months later but Zelda kept her last name. Larry was O.K. for a husband but she couldn't stand the idea of somebody calling her Mrs. King. Larry even learned two more Spanish words.

After about a year Zelda decided that she would like to live in Costa Rica. Larry agreed this was a great idea once he had established the fact that Costa Rica had race tracks.

In June of 2012 Larry and Zelda observed both their twentieth wedding anniversary and their twentieth year of living in Costa Rica. It had been a wonderful twenty years for both of them. Larry continued to lose money at the track but he had also learned to play golf. He had the most awkward swing in the history of the game, but while his partners in match play were laughing at his swing, Larry was winning hole after hole which compensated a little bit for his track losses. Larry also actually learned to speak Spanish but the only one he spoke it with was Zelda. Once a year or so he exchanged post cards with Vince who was the one person in the states with which he had any contact. Larry kept mum about just how he and Zelda were able to up and move to Costa Rica and Vince never asked. Vince did, in fact, become a bouncer at a hip club, met a cute chick there and was now a married man and a father. Moss, sadly, was murdered gangland style in 2004 for skimming. His family, however, was spared and in fact were financially secure as the result of provisions made for them by the same men who killed him. As Larry and Vince once agreed: rules are rules.

For her part, Zelda had picked out a beautiful home on the ocean for which she paid eight hundred thousand dollars in 1994. Her adroit investing skills had turned Larry's five million after taxes windfall into a considerable fortune. On the whole they lived rather modestly considering their economic status. A 1969 Rolls was about their only ostentatious possession. Zelda had started her second successful rug cleaning business but had retired in 2007 so she could devote her time to becoming a painter. Like every thing she touched, this opened up a whole new career for her and her paintings sold well wherever she displayed them. She never quibbled about Larry's track losses because she realized that no matter how terrible he was at picking horses he could never lose as much as the income from their investments.

One day Larry picked up the mail and felt his heart almost stop. Even after twenty years there was no mistaking the handwriting on the envelope. He waited until he got home before opening it. Inside was a letter, also handwritten.

Dear Mr. King:

Call me Ishmael. It's not my real name but it will do.

In 1992 my partner at the time, now my wife, and I were both twenty eight years old and working as secretaries for an insurance company in Newark, NJ. As was our custom, one Friday evening after work we stopped at our favorite bar to unwind and after three martinis began to talk like two teenagers about how we might escape the boring jobs we had and the chauvinistic bosses we worked for. Out popped the idea of winning a lottery. We decided to pick one with six numbers. We would use the number of letters in our first and last names for four of the numbers and we would try and find someone in the Newark phone directory whose names generated two new numbers. We opened the directory and there you were, providing us with a four and five. I'm sure you can guess the rest. Since you contributed we felt that you deserved a share, but we didn't want our identities known then and we still don't. We have lived in Vermont for many years and in 2011 we were married. As we celebrated we came up with the idea that we should at least resolve the mystery of that event which must have seemed so perplexing to you back in 1992. It was not easy to find you, but we have the financial resources available to hire people who do this sort of thing and this letter is the result. We hope these twenty years have been as pleasant for you as they have been for us.

Yours truly,
Ishmael

Larry read the letter to Zelda. For two or three minutes neither of them spoke.

Finally, Larry said, "I'm in shock."

"Do you want to give it back to them?" asked Zelda. "We can afford it and we can probably find them the same way they found you. But the letter makes it pretty clear that they want to be left alone."

"Ishmael. That's a pretty weird name, even for a les," said Larry.

"Larry, it's not a real name. It's the first line of a famous book by Herman Melville. The girl is sort of trying to make a joke."

"What's the book about?" asked Larry.

"A whale," answered Zelda, "and a guy's lifelong battle to find and kill it."

This revelation didn't do much to clear Larry's brain which seemed to be spinning in about six directions at once.

"Zelda, I got to do something worthwhile. I don't want to believe my whole life depended on dumb luck, the generosity of two girls and the fact that I married a smart chick."

"Larry, don't be so hard on yourself. If it wasn't for you, I'd still be cleaning rugs in Newark."

They discussed the situation for a couple of days. In the end they decided to do nothing but to plan to do something. For Zelda there was no problem. She was fully immersed in her painting. But Larry had a hard time.

About two weeks later Larry said, "Zelda, why don't we adopt some kids like those two movie stars, Brad something and Angelina? Maybe some kids from Somalia or China or some place."

Zelda thought a moment.

"Larry, what would you do with kids? You're fifty one years old."

"I'd teach them how to play the horses and win money playing golf. Besides, we could leave them a lot of dough," Larry replied. "I'll even read some books to them!"

"O.K. I'll think about it," said Zelda.

In fact, they did adopt two children. After some discussion they decided to name the boy Vince and the girl Sue Ann. Zelda accepted these choices without great enthusiasm but she had to admit they were certainly a lot better than Ishmael, which had been one of Larry's original choices.

A number of years later the family was having breakfast and Larry said, "Vince, tell your mother what you did at the track yesterday."

"I hit the trifecta, something Dad never did!" said Vince proudly as if he had just invented Facebook.

LUNCH AT LAHIERE'S

In 1953 my wife and I had been living in Princeton, New Jersey for about two years. One of the pleasures of living in Princeton was to enjoy meals at a restaurant on Witherspoon Street named Lahiere's. The restaurant was just a stone's throw from the campus of Princeton University and about a mile from the small home we had purchased when we first moved to Princeton from California in 1951. We had developed a casual routine of eating lunch about once a month at Lahiere's. The main dining area at Lahiere's was roughly a rectangle with tables along a wall which was mostly windows on one side, and another row of tables along the opposite side. Between these two rows were tables placed more or less randomly in the space between. About half way down the window side a structure ceiling high and about five feet by five feet square and been erected. This structure, covered with wood paneling, protruded into the main dining area and on the side facing the opposite wall there was a small table for two. Princeton lore had it that this table was always occupied by Albert Einstein when he visited the restaurant and it was, in fact, referred to as The Einstein Table. On the wall of the protruding structure above the table was a photograph of the great man himself.

No one seemed to know whether this story was true or whether it had been invented by the owner of Lahiere's, a man everyone called Mr. Christen. My wife and I had on a few occasions been seated at this very table, presumably on days when Professor Einstein was not expected.

One beautiful day in October my wife had gone to visit her family in Elizabeth, New Jersey and I decided to walk down to Lahiere's and have lunch there by myself. As the hostess led me into the room and to a table for two on the opposite side from the windows I was astonished to see Professor Einstein seated exactly where he should be, at the table bearing his name. I took my seat and tried, unsuccessfully, I'm afraid, to stop staring. After a few seconds the waitress who had been attending to Professor Einstein approached my table and said, "Professor Einstein would like you to join him at his table."

I was too flustered to reply coherently but managed "Ah . . . uh . . . o . . . o.k., thanks." And with that I stood up and walked the ten feet or so over to Einstein's table.

"Please sit down, young man," he said.

I did so, and he asked, "Why were you looking at me so intently?"

"Sir, you're the most famous man in the world and I've never seen you before. I guess I was startled."

"I'm not the most famous man in the world, just the most famous ex-patent clerk in the world," was his reply.

He then asked, "What is your name?"

"Neal Rosenberg."

"I'm a Jew," he said.

I expected him to add something more to this, but he didn't.

"I am aware of that sir and I assure you that Jewish people the world over are very proud of that fact and also are thankful for how much you supported them during the war." This worked as a thought but came out sounding ridiculous.

"Actually, I got out of Germany before Hitler got his hooks into me and really didn't have any real power here during the war to help anybody. Well, I suppose the letter helped some."

"Did you actually write that letter, sir?"

"No. It was written by some other physicists but they had me sign it because they were convinced I was the only physicist Roosevelt had ever heard of."

At this point the waitress asked if we were ready to order.

"I'll have the soup, salad and a glass of merlot." declared Einstein.

"Same for me," I said, trying to keep things as simple as possible.

When the waitress had left, he asked, "What are you doing here in Princeton?"

"I'm a member of the technical staff at RCA Laboratories," I replied.

"What do you do there?"

I explained that I was exploring the application of transistors to color television circuits.

"Television. I rarely watch it. There aren't many programs that appeal to me and it wastes a lot of time," he said.

He thought for a minute.

"However, I guess it's no more a waste of time than what I do, which is spend all day writing equations in a notebook trying to explain how the universe works."

He paused for a moment and seemed to reflect on the truth of what he had just said.

Our food arrived and we were quiet for a moment or two.

"Do you attend shul?" he finally asked.

"Not as often as I should," I replied. In truth I never attended shul but I was ashamed to admit as much.

"Me neither," he said. "But you can still be a good Jew, even if you don't attend shul."

Wanting to get off this subject as soon as I could I asked, "Do you always eat here by yourself?"

"No. I usually come with Gödel but he's in a snit today. We both play violin in our string quartet and last night when we were playing I'm afraid I hurt his feelings by pointing out to him that all his third position notes were out of tune."

"But you're normally very friendly with him. Isn't that so?"

"Yes. He is a brilliant man and the most interesting man I know when it comes to discussing weighty matters. Do you know that his world reputation rests on a theorem he proved when he was twenty five years old that there were a class of theorems that are impossible to prove?"

"I am aware of his work but, I must say, I don't understand it."

After a moment he continued, "He's a wonderful mathematician. Ten times better than I will ever be."

Another pause, and then "How old are you?" he asked.

"Thirty."

"Well, you better come up with something before another ten years. Creative mathematicians and physicists burn out after forty. I did my best work when I was below that age. As I got older I couldn't even understand some of the work being done by younger men and women. I still don't understand quantum mechanics and at one time I didn't even think it was correct. But the theory has stood up well over the years and repelled all attacks on it so far."

"Did you really say, 'God doesn't play dice with the universe.'?"

"Everybody says I did so I suppose I did. I'm an old man now and nobody want to embarrass me by bringing it up any more. But it appears that God does, indeed, do just that!"

"What do you think of the so-called big bang theory?" I asked.

"At first I didn't think it could be correct. But in 1935 I had some discussions with its first proponent, Monsignor Lemaitre, and he convinced me. In the end I don't think it matters very much how the universe started or how it will end. No one was there at the beginning and we will all be gone by the end."

The wine had made me a little bolder, so I asked, "How old were you when you first realized you were a genius?"

"People started using that term to describe me around 1905 when I published my special theory. At the time they said that only ten people in the world understood what I was saying. Anytime you come up with something that baffles a lot of the population they start referring to you as either a genius or a lunatic. I would guess it was about half and half back in those days. It helps too, if you never comb your hair!"

"Do you think you will succeed in developing your unified theory?" I asked.

"Not likely I'm afraid. I'm probably too old now. But somebody, or more probably, some group of people will someday."

"Besides yourself, who would you classify as a genius?"

"My first choice would be Newton. You can write all of Newton's laws and equations on a postcard and they tell you everything anybody needs to know about force, acceleration, gravity and motion. Newton's laws explain how the entire solar system works, how to predict eclipses, the tides and a host of other things that we experience every day. They are easy to verify with simple experiments. It's only when you get to the tenth decimal point or so that you need my stuff. It took them years and the careful measurement of the bending of starlight by the sun during an eclipse before my prediction this would happen could be verified. You don't need relativity to know that if you drop a bowling ball on your foot you're probably going to break a toe," he concluded.

The waitress arrived to take our order for dessert. Einstein chose chocolate mousse and coffee and, as before, I ordered the same.

"Do you think that there are other living creatures outside our solar system?" I asked.

"It's difficult to say. There are billions of galaxies and billions of stars in each galaxy so I think the laws of probability would lead one to believe so. The trouble is, if there are any, they're so far away we'll never be able to see them with our own eyes. We may hear from them by radio waves but I think that is unlikely too. This is more a question for religion or philosophy than it is for science."

Our desserts arrived and we were once again silent.

Having gotten this far without antagonizing him, I decided to press on into some more personal areas.

"You have been described as a pacifist. Is that true?" I inquired.

"Yes. I became one after the senseless carnage of the first war. In the twenties and early thirties there were a lot of us. But then when Hitler arrived and it was clear that he was going to lead Germany into war many of us had to revise our position. I still think wars never really resolve any problems in the long run but I guess we're stuck with them for the foreseeable future. My greatest fear is that we will blow ourselves up before we figure out how to avoid them."

I expected this response so I switched gears again.

"Do you think that anti-Semitism is a problem for Jews today?"

"Anti-Semitism has always been a problem for Jews and so it is today. It has simmered down in the United States for the time being. There are prominent Jews in all walks of life here and we have certainly won our share of Nobel Prizes. But we must be wary. At one time there was more anti-Semitism in Poland and France than in Germany. But, as we saw there, things can change very quickly."

I felt I had taken enough of his time discussing rather serious subjects so I decided to lighten up a little.

"Are you ever bothered by people here in Princeton asking for your autograph or requesting that you pose for pictures, that sort of thing?"

"Not so much anymore. When I first came here I was more of a curiosity than I am now. People in Princeton are a little on the blasé side and there are many other well-known persons who live here. I am not a Professor at Princeton. My affiliation is with the Advanced Institute which is not very near the campus and a little off the beaten track. Once in a while someone comes to the door of my home on Mercer Street but my housekeeper generally handles the situation and I don't have to make an appearance."

"If you hadn't been a physicist what would you have liked to be?" I asked.

"That's easy. A musician. As I think I told you, I'm a pretty good violinist."

He paused a moment and then asked, "By the way, are you married?"

"Yes sir, I am."

"Well, I hope you have better luck than I did!"

He then looked at his watch and said, "Well, I must be on my way. I've got to find Gödel and patch things up. He's the best friend I have and I don't want him to stay mad too long."

With that Einstein rose, said goodbye and strolled out of the restaurant onto Witherspoon Street and headed toward Nassau Street, presumably to find his friend Gödel. I was happy to pay the bill for the lunch. Einstein had the reputation for being a little absent minded but I prefer to think the wily professor had invited me over so he could get a free lunch!

It's been fifty nine years since the most memorable meal of my life. When I got home, I wrote some notes down but I never told anybody about it until now. I thought then that everybody would think I was making it all up and that I had too fertile an imagination. Probably some people who read this now will think the same thing.

Later that evening my wife asked, "How was your lunch?"

"The usual," I said.

MOVIE REVIEWS

KNOCKED UP

If you can weather a veritable hurricane of F-words you might enjoy "Knocked Up", a film that sort of tries to address a fairly serious problem in a fairly serious but also comic way. The plot is simplicity itself. Allison (Katherine Heigl) is a "behind the camera" employee of the TV show E! who early in the film receives a promotion to be an "on camera" employee. To celebrate this momentous event, she and her married sister, Debbie (Leslie Mann) visit a hip night spot where Allison strikes up a conversation with Ben (Seth Rogen). After a few too many drinks Ben and Allison end up in bed and due to some poor communication skills make love without benefit of condom protection. The next morning they separate with little expectation that they will ever see one another again.

A few weeks later while Allison is performing her new "on camera" role with vigor she experiences a couple of those rather indelicate symptoms of morning sickness. In one of the more comic scenes in the movie Allison and her sister Debbie frantically buy about a dozen pregnancy kits in a drugstore and try all of them out in a desperate attempt to find a negative result. Alas, it is not to be and Allison contacts Ben and informs him that she is indeed pregnant and he is the papa. Ben's immediate response to this news is about 20 F-words but he eventually settles down and like the good guy he really is agrees to help her in any way he can.

We learn that Ben has no money and no regular job but that he and four of his buddies are developing a web site which when one enters the name of a movie star will provide all the movies in which he or she but mostly she appears nude as well as the exact locations time wise in the movie where these scenes occur. Allison seems to accept this information without undue stress although it does appear to be a somewhat fragile occupation for her baby's father.

They finally go to see a doctor together and the doctor, with the aid of an instrument that resembles a dildo, shows them an ultrasound image of their 8 week old heir with its little heart happily beating away, a scene that should convert at least half the audience to a pro-life stance if they don't already have one.

As a diversion from the saga of Ben and Allison, we are treated to the trials and tribulations of Debbie and Pete's marriage which is useful in showing Ben just what he has in store for him in the future. Debbie and Pete (Paul Rudd) have two adorable little girls of their own. In a male bonding episode, when Ben and Pete go off to Las Vegas together, we are treated to some rather trite observations about how marriage and children sort of limit a man's options like going off to live in India for a year.

Soon, however, we are yanked back to the primary story line which, of course, leads to the main event-the birth of the baby (a girl) and an ending where everybody is feeling pretty good and Ben and Allison are driving down an LA freeway to their new abode right out of "My Blue Heaven".

All the actors discharge their responsibilities admirably and the four principals each have their chance to grab the lime light for a time. Mr. Rogen comes across as a decent sort who tries his best to step up to his responsibilities. Miss Mann also has some juicy scenes, particularly one in which she dukes it out with a doorman at a night club who insists that she and Allison go to the end of the line of people waiting to get in because she is too old and her sister is 8 months' pregnant and he can't give them special treatment to go in immediately. Mr. Rudd discharges his duties competently although there are times when he seems to wonder how he ever wandered into this movie.

But the real star of the story is Allison. As portrayed by Miss Heigl, she is a fairly complex woman who handles her predicament with the full knowledge that she is in a tough spot but convinces herself that she is up to handling it. In the two sex scenes with Ben she doesn't seem to be enjoying herself very much and is constantly shouting instructions to him as he tries desperately to please her. The only time she appears near orgasm is when she is informed by her boss at E! of her promotion. Although constantly surrounded by a barrage of F-words fluttering around her pretty head, Miss Heigl reacts as if she were listening to the weather report on a particularly nice day. However, she appears to be totally overwhelmed by modesty when it comes down to exposing any part of her anatomy of any interest to men. In both love scenes her brassiere remains fully on and in the one bathtub scene her breasts remain discreetly covered with soap foam while her 9 month pregnant belly protrudes about 8 inches out of the water. It appears that Miss Heigl will never be seen on Ben's web site.

In the birth scene, which is about as realistic as has ever been portrayed on the silver screen, she stays right in character as she bosses the attending doctor around in much the same way as she does Ben during their love making.

Debbie and Pete's five year old daughter doesn't get a chance to utter the F-word but she does manage one "prick" when she asks Ben what it means, as in "he's a prick". In one of the funniest lines of the movie Ben informs her with an absolutely straight face that it means penis to which she responds as though she has finally stumbled upon the true meaning of life, as perhaps she has.

THE LAST SEDUCTION

Here's the scene: A group of old pros who had written, directed and produced movies in Hollywood in the 1930's are sitting around a table in one of the lounges in Heaven reminiscing about making pictures in those days and particularly the problems they encountered when confronted with the censors who administered the so-called Production Code, which at that time was very strict indeed about what constituted suitable material to be depicted in movies. Finally one of the gentleman speaks up and says: "Listen, why don't we dream up a movie where *every* scene in the movie would be in violation of the code! Today we could probably get it a PG13 or at worst an R!". Well, if they were to carry out this idea, the movie they have in mind would come quite close to being "The Last Seduction", certainly the most noir of any film noir I've seen to date. The heroine, if I can stretch the definition of the term, is a woman named Bridget Gregory (brilliantly played by Linda Fiorentino) who, when the movie starts, is waiting in their New York City apartment for her husband, Clay, (played by Bill Pullman) to return from a major drug deal. He does so, with about $700,000 stuffed in his shirt because the buyers of the drugs had dumped all the money from the brief case in which they brought it on the ground and calmly strolled off with the drugs and one extra brief case. Bridget seems suitably impressed and Clay retires to the bath room to take a shower after which he promises her they will celebrate. While he is in the shower, Bridget fills another bag with a roll of paper towels and leaves with the bag containing the money. Clay emerges from his shower and is not too happy to discover that his wife is gone, as is the money, and all he has to show for the afternoon's work in a roll of paper towels.

Bridget travels upstate to a small town where she gets a room in a motel, lands a job with an insurance company, changes her name to Wendy Kroy (New York backwards, sort of) and allows herself to be picked up in a bar by a young fellow named Mike Swale (Peter Berg) who has just returned to his home town from Buffalo where he had gone to make his fortune but instead had entered into a bad marriage. They begin a relationship like that between a spider and a fly-she's the spider and he's the fly. Clay, meanwhile, is really getting annoyed because he needs some of the money to pay off a debt he has incurred with some apparently impatient and nasty people. He guesses her new name because he is aware of her ability to write backwards and hires a private detective to find her and force her to relinquish the money. The detective (Bill Nunn) finds her but she outsmarts him and disposes of him in a rather creative way indeed.

Mike, obviously besotted with this beautiful sexy girl wants their relationship to expand into something more than just sexual bouts but about this time we begin to sense that Bridget has a long range plan which includes getting much richer than she already is, permanently getting rid of Clay and using this rube from the sticks to help her carry out her plan and then disposing of him as well. As Mike gets more and more entangled in her bizarre schemes he is torn between his overwhelming sexual attraction to her and his realization that this Wendy Kroy is the most morally depraved person he has ever met. It would not be fair to reveal whether Bridget succeeds in her plan, or if she does, what the future holds for her. You'll have to see the film if you want to find out.

The film does not violate the old Production Code in *every* scene but it does have graphic sex, nudity, endless swear words, unpunished crimes, a brief allusion to male homosexuality, sexual innuendo between a white women and a black man, and drug dealing by a licensed physician plus the moral depravity of its heroine.

The acting is first rate throughout and Miss Fiorentino should have won an Oscar for her effort. The direction by John Dahl is also flawless although some sensitive souls may be put off by some of the rather nasty violence near the picture's end.

My taste is probably a little weird but I enjoyed this movie a lot. In particular, I was fascinated by Bridget's relentless efforts to achieve her goals with no regard whatsoever for normally accepted moral principles.

Returning for a moment to our friends up there in Heaven we find that they have been joined by their old adversary, Mr. Joe Breen, who was the most ardent enforcer of the old Production Code. Mr. Breen has made the mistake of seeing this movie and is suffering from a very severe attack of apoplexy, assuming one can have apoplexy in Heaven.

ONCE

Most movies that attempt to combine romance with musical achievement fail to succeed on one count or the other; sometimes both. "Once" is a film that has romance and musical achievement and is absolutely convincing from start to finish. Made in Ireland, it tells the story of a guy, played by Glen Hansard, who works part time in his father's vacuum cleaner repair shop and part time as a street musician playing his guitar and singing for coins on the streets of Dublin. One day a girl, played by Markéta Irglová, passes by as she is trying to sell some magazines and compliments him on his musical efforts. They strike up a conversation and we learn that it just so happens that she has a Hoover that is in need of repair. He tells her to bring it tomorrow and he will repair it for her in his father's shop. The next day she shows up pulling the Hoover by it's long hose like it is a dog on a leash. On their way to the shop she invites him to stop at a music store where the proprietor is kind enough to let her practice on one of the grand pianos he has there for sale. She plays a piece and it is immediately obvious to both the guy and to us that she is very talented indeed. He asks her if she would like to learn a song he has written and throws the lyrics up on the piano. He plays the intro on his guitar and she picks up on the song gradually on the piano and also sings the song with him in harmony. To me, this is the most moving scene in the film as they both begin to realize that they are musically compatible and, as the song proceeds, they also feel something else but they're not quite sure what it is. The song is "Falling Slowly" which won the Oscar for 2007 as the best song in a film and in fact was written by Irglová and Hansard.

We soon learn that neither of them is as unencumbered as they first appear. He still pines for his girlfriend who has left him and moved to London and she, who is a Czech immigrant, lives with her mother and her three year old daughter although her husband is not in Dublin but home in the Czech Republic. Despite the dampening effect this has on any possible romance, they decide to collaborate musically, write some songs and perhaps make a CD. They assemble three more musicians and after bargaining with the owner of a recording studio (an entertaining scene in its own right) they arrive at the studio where they are left in the care of a recording engineer masterfully played by Geoff Minogue. It is obvious immediately to him that these kids are rank amateurs and he is clearly bored to death with having to spend his weekend teaching them the basic rudiments of recording. He finally gets them set up and they make their first track. As the music progresses, without saying a word, the recording engineer begins to realize that, green as they are, their music is something special. The transformation from blasé spectator to full participant in the session by the recording engineer is just one of the many winning performances in this film. After many hours everybody is exhausted but satisfied that they have accomplished something important. After they have listened to the last track the recording engineer warns them that they have been listening to their efforts on very good studio speakers and the real test is how they will sound on "shitty" speakers. They all pile into his Mercedes station wagon whose audio system apparently meets his criteria, a nice touch, and off they go to the sea shore where they frolic like children, which for the moment they are.

The movie contains a number of vignettes which don't necessarily move the action along but help to flesh out the simple story.

In one of these the guy composes a song in his small home studio while we are treated to images he recorded with a video camera of his departed girlfriend when they were together and in love. In another the girl is listening to a CD when the batteries run out in her Walkman and, after discovering that the TV remote has no batteries in it, "borrows" some money from her daughter's piggy bank so she can go buy some new batteries, promising her that she'll pay her back as soon as she can.

The guy and the girl make a date for what promises to be a sexual encounter but the girl has second thoughts and never comes. In a marvelous scene which actually takes only about a minute but seems like hours he waits for her and waits for her but finally gives up when he realizes she is not going to come after all.

The film ends quietly. The guy decides to fly to London and try to reclaim his lost love but before he leaves he borrows some money from his father and has a piano delivered to the girl's apartment. At the end of the movie we are allowed to peak into her third floor apartment where she is enjoying her new piano and her husband, returned from the Czech Republic, plays with his daughter, a scene of such warmth that we are moved; corny as it is.

The performances by all the actors is superb, as is the direction by John Carney. All the songs played in the movie were actually written, played and sung by Hansard and Irglová.

This film is a gem. See it!

HUMOR

A MONOLOGUE FOR AN OLD STAND UP COMIC

Hi . . . I know what you're all thinking: Why is a seventy year old gentleman like me trying to make seven people laugh when I could be home watching porno movies on cable TV?

Well, my mother wanted to know the same thing when she called me from Las Vegas last week. She also asked me why I didn't get a decent job like pushing drugs or pimping. Don't laugh. She clears $1000 a night with just three girls!

Anyway, my problems started when I was in first grade on Valentine's Day. All the other boys got valentines but me . . . . well, that isn't quite true . . . it's just that my valentines said stuff like "YOU STINK . . . GET LOST . . . YOU'RE A JERK" . . . Well, you get the gist.

I decided that I would never get a girl if I didn't get to be a star at something. I looked around and decided I would learn to play the trumpet like a guy named Harry James. He was married to just about the most luscious movie star of all time named Betty Grable so I figured if I could learn to play "You Made me Love You" like Harry James maybe I could get a girl like that too. My folks bought me a trumpet and I took lessons and practiced about twelve hours a day and before you know it I could play "You Made Me Love You" just like Harry James.

I'm sorry to say that it didn't work out. The problem was that Harry James was about fifteen inches taller than I was and even though I stood up when I played "You Made Me Love You" all the girls thought I was sitting down and Harry James NEVER played "You Made Me Love You" sitting down!

I thought, well maybe I just picked the wrong instrument so I tried piano. Everybody knew that girl singers were in love with their accompanists so I studied piano and learned how to play all the pop tunes in the weird keys that girl singers always choose. Some girl singer would say, "Body and Soul in B" and I would say, "OK sweetheart, no problem", and off we would go. I'm probably the only piano player who ever played "Body And Soul" in the key of B. But alas, it didn't do any good. After accompanying seventeen girls in every weird key that you can imagine I still hadn't got even one of them to go to bed with me.

By that time I was forty years old and still hadn't got a girl to make love with me. In fact, I was the model for that movie they made a couple of years ago.

Since I had struck out with musical approaches, I decided to give sports a try. At that time a chick by the name of Chris Evert was not only the best woman tennis player in the world but also one of sexiest women around. So I took up tennis figuring that if I could get into the US Open when she was in it I could meet her and let nature take its course. My tennis technique was a little strange because I used the two-handed grip for all my shots, including the serve. However, I finally managed to get into the Open as the 476th seed but I was defeated in the first round by a twelve year old girl from Albania. I don't know if the officials thought she was a boy or that I was a girl. At any rate, I never got to meet Chris Evert but I did watch her on television while dreaming what might have been.

I failed at music and sports but I took heart when I saw a stand up comic by the name of Woody Allen in a couple of movies. Mr. Allen was short and almost as ugly as I was and yet he had all those cool chicks like Diane Keaton and Mia Farrow. So anyway, now you know why I'm up here trying to make seven people laugh.

Odyssey Records Inc.
36 West 47th St.
New York, NY 01009

Ms. Shahyra
26354 Wisteria Terrace
Long Beach, CA 91453

Dear Ms. Shahyra:

Thank you so much for sending us your Demo CD of Hoagy Carmichal's immortal *Stardust*. I think my partners and I can say without a doubt that, although we have heard at least 24 renditions of this beautiful song, we have never heard one remotely resembling yours. We do, however, have a few minor suggestions for your consideration.

It would probably be a good idea for you to spruce up your intonation slightly. Of the 126 notes in Mr. Carmichael's lovely ballad we found that only 19 of the notes you sang were within 1/4 tone of the note specified by Mr. Carmichael. We must admit though, that although it startles the ear somewhat on first hearing, that you certainly deserve an A+ for an innovative performance intonation-wise.

Your choice of tempo, one quarter note per minute, is certainly state of the art for unusual meter but it results in taking 2 hours and 8 minutes for a single chorus of the song, which possibly may exceed the attention span of many of our listeners. We have sold many copies of our boxed set of CDs which contains Richard Wagner's entire Ring cycle of 4 operas and if played in total takes just over 22 hours. But what we have found is that nobody actually listens to more than the first 7 minutes of Das Rhinegold (the first opera in the cycle) before replacing it with something like The Mamas and the Papas *California Dreaming*.

Your decision to sing the song in Swahili may reduce your potential audience in the U.S. but it certainly should help you develop a following in Africa.

With respect to your cover photo we feel that you may be pushing the envelope just a bit here. The picture of the nude girl apparently giving birth to a corn cob is an obvious reference to the terrible rape of Temple Drake in the novel *Sanctuary* by William Faulkner. Mr. Faulkner is, of course, one of America's greatest writers and a winner of the Nobel Prize in literature and honoring him is certainly an appropriate thing to do. But we feel that this particular choice may be a little too raunchy for the target demographic for our records which is 7-11 year old girls.

In general we are a very conservative company and our biggest stars are conventional artists like Bjork. Perhaps it would be worth your while to submit your CD to a more radical record producer such as RCA Victor Red Seal.

Your very truly,
Angel Bronstein,
Executive Producer

PRESIDENTIAL QUOTATIONS

Many of our great presidents have produced memorable quotations. Here are a few of them. See if you can name the president who said:

1. "Yes, I cut down the cherry tree because I couldn't stand looking at those damned pink cherry blossoms every May!"
2. (Inaugural address) "We have nothing to fear but 50 million Krauts, 40 million Japs, the worst depression in history and Bonnie and Clyde!"
3. (To speech writer) "What the fuck does fourscore mean?"
4. (Television address) "I am not a child molester . . . er . . . . I mean crook!"
5. "Jackie, for the last time, I am not screwing Marilyn Monroe! Now get in the car. I don't want to be late for our flight to Dallas!"
6. "Honey, maybe you should soft pedal the singing for a while and try writing mystery novels."
7. "Monica, are you sure the oval office is really the most appropriate place for what you're doing at the present time?"
8. "I'm sorry Sally, but it just doesn't look presidential for me to have little pickaninnies running around the White House all the time!".

9. "Look guys, I'm going to take a breather. You charge up the god-damned hill!"

10. (At ICBM negotiations). "Gorby, I'll tell you what. You show me yours and I'll show you mine!"

ROSES AND THORNS

A MEMOIR

PREFACE

Writing a memoir is a rather childish and self-centered thing to do, yet many people do it, even ordinary people like me. One of the reasons that I attempted to write one is that I wish my grandparents and parents had done so. While parents know a lot about their children's lives, at least until they grow up, children know only what they remember about their parents and grandparents unless they have some source to refer to after their parents and grandparents have passed away. Of course, it's possible that my descendants will have no interest in what happened to me in my eighty-seven years but, if that is the case, it won't matter to me because I'll be gone.

I decided that, rather than a chronological approach, I would organize the story by subject. If a particular subject bores you, you can always skip to the next subject.

This is not a "tell all" story. I have omitted those events that might embarrass any living person or, for that matter, embarrass the reader.

A memoir is not an autobiography, which requires documentation. The author of a memoir has only the obligation to tell his story truthfully as he remembers it.

FAMILY

It seems to me that I had both an unusual and a very mundane family. The further one tries to go back, the more unusual. By the time one gets to my parents, everything is routine. On my father's side I can only go back as far as his mother. I never knew my paternal grandfather at all and nobody ever talked that much about him. But my paternal grandmother, Mary Lohman, was a bit unusual herself. Apparently deserted by her husband, she took up a career as a seamstress and she was very good at her craft. She also managed to carry on a liaison with a married man for years by the name of Frank. I never saw much of Frank and my mother disapproved of him in a big way but at least he didn't just disappear like my grandfather. My brother Dirk and I sometimes spent time staying with Mary during the summer when we were young and my memory of those times is that she offered very little discipline and was generally fun to be around. There was one story that she told many times that I remember. She had made a satiny dress for a young girl and the girl complained that the outline of her underpants showed through the dress. Mary tried a number of fixes and when none of them worked she suggested that the solution was for the girl to simply not wear any underpants. That solved the problem!

Mary spent her last years in a nursing home with my maternal grandmother, Goldie Inskeep.

On my mother's side I can go back to her grandmother, Fannie Booher. By the time I knew her, her husband, a harness maker, had passed away but Fannie was very much alive and well. Fannie had 5 children, 3 of which survived beyond infancy, my great aunt Bertha, my great uncle Aniel and my grandmother Goldie. Bertha was stricken with polio when young but managed to live a productive life even though she carried the effects of that disease the rest of her life. She was not really disabled, but needed a cane to walk. The most important result of her bad luck was probably the difficulty a young girl had in those days of finding a husband if one had even the slightest disability. Bertha was a gifted painter and a joy to be around. Fannie lived to the age of 93 and would probably still be here if she hadn't fallen and broken her hip. She was a tough old girl and Dirk and I quaked if she got on our case about anything. She had roast chicken every Sunday for dinner and she raised the chickens herself and executed them in her own style when it was time to cook them. She loved her great grandchildren but a story that I remember is that when someone asked her if she wasn't sad when we left, she replied "Yes, but it's a good sad!"

Goldie's husband, Carlos, is probably the most interesting of all my relatives. Carlos was an actor and when he was playing in the small town of Darlington, Indiana, he stole my 17-year old grandmother and spirited her off to become an actress, which, in fact, she became. Eventually my mother was the result of this union and, in the style of my grandfathers, Carlos took off for greener or most probably younger pastures. I did see him once when he took Dirk and me on a boat trip around Manhattan. He was a handsome devil and was probably a scam artist in addition to being an actor. His name was not really Inskeep, what it was I don't know. I always liked the name and I thought it was quite rare. But when I tried to find Carlos it turned out that there were a million Inskeeps in the U.S.

Everybody always said that Dirk resembled Carlos and the very limited photographic evidence we have supports that allegation. Goldie was a very interesting girl too. She and Carlos were in many plays together, some of which also included my mother, billed as "Baby Frances". In 1964 I appeared in a play that the three of them had acted in those many years ago called "Ten Nights In a Bar Room". For years she made a living by demonstrating Murphy's Oil Soap at the Marshall Fields department store in Chicago. She was so good at it that she was on a first name basis with Mr. Murphy himself.

She also ran a rooming house which had as tenants actors and other show business people. One of these, a circus strong man named Orville Stamm, had an act with two beautiful young ladies which was sort of a dance and showed off Orville's strength as well. At the act's climax Orville lifted a platform containing the two girls and a full grown horse off the ground while lying prone on the stage floor. Orville was also an inventor and he finally married one of the two girls after living with her at Goldie's place for a number of years. Her name was Martha and I had a terrible crush on her when I was about 8 years old. But I was no competition for Orville.

Goldie was unusual in another way. In her time, and among people like her contemporaries, she had absolutely no biases. I never heard her say a word against Jews, blacks, gays or any other group. She also accepted Orville and Martha's unmarried cohabitation without comment. Considering the time in which she lived, this was remarkable.

My father Harry's early life is opaque to me. The first time he appears is when he married my mother. They apparently met when they were students at Crane College. My guess is that Crane was a 2 year school and so neither my father nor my mother graduated from a 4 year program. My father was good looking and cut a somewhat dashing figure in the 1920's. He started his career at a very low level with the Western Electric Company at the Hawthorn Plant in Chicago. In 1929 he was transferred to the plant in Kearny, NJ and we took up residence in Cranford, NJ in a rented house on South Central Avenue. My earliest memory is of one Christmas at this location when I received a Lionel electric train from my parents. It was typical of them to shield me and Dirk from the awful depression which began just when we moved to NJ. Despite the depression, my father kept getting promoted at Western Electric and we began a series of moves to better and better neighborhoods in Cranford. Our next home was at 26 Arlington Rd. in Cranford and there are a few memories I have of our time there. When I was 11 or so I contracted scarlet fever which in those days was considered a serious disease. Our home was quarantined and I was isolated from the rest of our family to the extent that this was possible. Our next door neighbor was an old lady with a daughter named Corrine Belden. Ms. Belden was not married and, as far as I know, was never married. She was, however, an excellent pianist and my parents decided that I should take lessons from her. It was her custom to paste gold stars on a pupil's lesson if he or she did well in learning a lesson.

After 6 months I had received not one single gold star and my parents decided that maybe I should leave piano playing to the more gifted.

Corrine had a sort of boyfriend named Johnny Critenden. Johnny was very good looking and much younger than my mother. But even at an early age, probably around 12 or so, I noticed that Johnny spent an awful lot of time with my mother. I don't know what the basis was for their relationship but nobody seemed unduly upset about it. Certainly not my father who was responsible for getting a job for Johnny at Western Electric where he spent his entire career. Everybody in my parent's circle expected that Johnny would marry Corrine. Then, as a complete surprise to everyone, one day Johnny showed up married to a young, sexy girl named Jean. Everybody was shocked, shocked at this betrayal but, as it turned out, Jean and Johnny were married until Johnny died and they became lifelong friends of my parents. My father continued to rise at Western and ended up a Vice President of the company. He held many jobs during his career there but the one he loved was as Western manager of the Dew Line which was the first line to detect Soviet missiles and was built near the Arctic Circle. My father spent a lot of time out of the country on this job hobnobbing with military brass and clearly enjoyed the perks such as his own private plane, etc. My father was a legend at Western. I worked there for two summers when I was going to college and if anybody found out I was Harry's son I was accorded special status indeed. It seemed that everybody in that company knew and admired Harry Lohman.

My father was not a particularly articulate man and he tended to teach by example. He was certainly a "company" man but he also had tremendous empathy for other types of people. He especially liked men who earned a living working with their hands such as carpenters and other men who built houses. He seemed to have a real feel for those who were less fortunate than he was and he tried to teach me to be compassionate, not by lecturing to me, but by example. His relationship with my mother certainly had its ups and downs but I am sure he loved her and he showed it, not by pretty phrases, but, as a typical example, buying her a beautiful grand piano at the height of the depression, a piano I own now. But he had a romantic side as well. Every Valentine's Day for over thirty years he composed a poem and sent it to my first wife, Ethel. All in all, I would say that I was very fortunate in having a father like Harry Lohman.

My mother's early life is also a mystery to me. When she was very young she acted in plays with my grandfather and grandmother but she was really raised by her grandmother and her aunt Bertha. She was a very beautiful young girl and I am sure attracted many boys within the rather limited pool at Darlington. But, in the end, she married my father whom she met at college. My mother was not an easy person to know. She was opinionated and stubborn but she could also be extremely charming and had a host of friends. I know that my father was very proud of her, especially when she was required to appear at company events where she always acquitted herself in an admirable manner. She was even handed in the treatment of my brother and me and though in later years she became more involved in my brother's affairs than in mine it was because his affairs were much more complicated than mine.

Many years after he was married she kept in contact with one of his old girlfriends whom I believe she would have preferred as a daughter-in-law.

My mother had all the biases normal for a person of her time and background but one of her best friends until the day she died was a black maid who worked for her.

Although she was very strict in sexual matters, at least after she got older, she could be fooled by a clever talker. When I was 17 I was playing at a notorious Mafia night club by the name of Princess Wanas, (More of this in the music section of this tale) my mother was very dubious about this job but one of the other musicians by the name of Pete Billias who was about five years older than I completely conned her into believing that he would take care of me and make sure that I didn't do anything for which she wouldn't approve. Of course, this was all bullshit since Pete made every effort that he could to lead me astray, but he sure fooled my mother. Pete was a Greek and though he wasn't handsome at all he had those soulful eyes that could melt the resistance of any woman, including my mother.

My mother was musical. She could sing and was a gifted pianist. She was especially good at sight reading a piano piece although she couldn't play a single song by ear. She was very proud of my accomplishments on the trumpet and in college. But I had the feeling that as she grew older she became slightly bitter with the realization that she had given up many career opportunities in order to be a very good wife and mother. She was unlucky to be born just at the time when women went from being slaves to their husbands and children to the era when women began to realize that they could be much more. If she had been born in 1940 instead of 1902 I think her life might have been much different.

Over the years I have heard many people complain about their parents. I have no such complaints. I never thought that they acted poorly where I was concerned and I always looked up to them and respected them. My only regret is that I never really knew them. My brother, Dirk, was three years younger than I and these three years made it difficult for us to establish a relationship when we were young. At 18 I joined the army and Dirk and I never lived close to one another again. Our personalities were very different and we followed different career paths. Dirk resembled Carlos in that girls loved him while I struggled to find a girl who would even date me. While I was following a rather mundane path as an engineer, Dirk was an agent of the CIA in France. Dirk spoke perfect French and Russian and the biggest disappointment in his life was when the CIA refused to keep him in France and transferred him stateside. His first marriage broke up and he married a girl named Nancy whom he met when they both worked for a French translation service in Seattle. His second marriage lasted until he died and in his later years I think he was happy and enjoyed both his first and second family, especially his four children and their children. We also became closer in late life and would have been even closer if we had lived nearer to each other.

When I was young, I was preoccupied with my own life and paid scant attention to my family roots. It is something I regret. I wish they had all written a memoir like this that I could read every so often to remind me where I came from.

WORK

I had a lot of different jobs over the years but in this section I'll cover only those which were non-musical. A job that I really liked I had when I was 16 years old. It was delivering groceries for McMahon's Market. After school I would report to the store and make up boxes of the groceries that I was to deliver later that afternoon. When all the boxes were full, I loaded them into a truck and began the deliveries. It was a high prestige job because of the driving and I enjoyed every minute of it. I wish I could say that one of the young married women where I delivered the groceries invited me in and tried to seduce me, but, alas, it never happened. I also had a number of jobs mowing lawns and delivering magazines which were uneventful at best. At college, during the summers after my sophomore and junior years I had a job at the Western Electric Company. It was obvious that I would never have had these jobs if it hadn't been for my father but I tried my best to acquit myself in a useful manner and I think I was successful in doing this. These jobs gave me valuable experience working in a real engineering environment and also gave me the opportunity to emulate my father by commuting every day on the Jersey Central Railroad to Kearny, NJ. By that time my father was working at AT&T headquarters at 195 Broadway in NY but, as I already mentioned, everybody at Kearny knew him and my path there was smooth indeed. After I graduated from Norwich University in Northfield Vermont I worked the summer before I went to North Carolina for graduate work for the Northfield Power Company. This was a two-man operation and me. We did everything from changing street lights to running new lines to houses which were just getting electricity for the first time. It was hard work and I loved it. We dug new pole holes by hand and pulled a new pole into the hole with just one man on the winch and the other two making sure the pole didn't swing as it was lowered into the hole. The two men were Harry and Gene. Harry was leery of college boys and I took a lot of hazing from him. Gene, however was extremely kind to me and taught me a lot about being a power lineman. He showed me how to climb poles with hooks ("keep your ass out or you'll slide down and break your neck!"), how to drill holes in a newly installed pole for the cross bars while standing on hooks and supported by a belt and many other tricks of the trade. I fell only once while climbing, almost certainly because I didn't "keep my ass out!" Harry drew the line at letting me work on 2300 volt lines but I did a lot of work on 220 and 110 volt lines when they were hot. I became very fond of these two guys and, even now, I have tremendous admiration for power company linemen.

When I was at graduate school in North Carolina I worked one summer for the Electrical Engineering Dept. moving the Engineering Lab to a new building. There was lots of heavy equipment that had to be moved and the professor and I who performed the job had only the most rudimentary moving machinery to move it. There was no air conditioning of any kind and North Carolina summers are HOT. I remember coming home each day and tumbling right from the shower into bed I was so tired.

In June of 1951 I was hired by RCA Laboratories in Princeton, N.J. I was very lucky to get this job. The RCA Laboratories was a very high prestige place but a combination of my excellent grades at North Caroline State and my bluffing my way through the tough interview process got me the job.

In those days new hires at the Laboratories were required to serve 3 4-month assignments with different groups so that they could see what type of work they wanted to do and also for the Labs to see if they wanted to keep the applicant at all. I enjoyed all three of my assignments and was offered a position with all three. But on my third assignment I really lucked out. It was with a Staff Member by the name of George Szklai, a Hungarian who was a genius for having novel ideas but couldn't solder two wires together. In November of 1952 RCA was planning to give a seminar to all it's licensees to show them that RCA was a leader in transistor technology (at that time RCA made about $100 million a year from licensing its patents). George had the idea to make a transistorized TV set using no vacuum tubes except for the picture tube. Everybody thought he was crazy because transistors had not yet progressed to the point where they could handle the requirements of TV circuitry. But George persisted and put the task to me and Gerry Herzog, a new member of the staff hired the same day as I was. Gerry and I split the various circuits required to make a TV and during the summer we often worked 80 hours a week trying to make transistors do the work for which they were not really qualified. We had a lot of help from the transistor research group and they supplied us with experimental transistors which eventually made it possible for us to achieve our goal. The TV set we made had only a 3 inch screen and could receive only one channel but it was the first of its kind ever and we demonstrated it to the licensees and the press about 50 times without a single failure. We published our results in the Proceedings of the IEEE and for a while we were world famous. Although the set was not practical at all it still was of great interest to everybody because it signified that the days of the vacuum tube were about to end. This TV set is now at the Smithsonian Institute in Washington, DC.

The project made stars of Gerry and me and for a time I thought that research was going to be my life's work. But after about five years I began to realize that I simply didn't have the ability to be an outstanding researcher. There were too many really brilliant people at the Labs and although I knew all of them and was treated well by all of them I knew I could never be one of them. So in 1956 when I was offered a job in the newly created RCA Semiconductor Division in Somerville, N.J. I accepted it. In Somerville the competition was much easier and I progressed there quickly, first as a technical engineer and then, through a series of promotions, to management. By 1965 I was in charge of about 50 engineers and reported to the head of the Integrated Circuit Division, a fellow by the name of Lloyd Day. Lloyd was a smart guy but he was not technically trained and tended to worry more about the politics of RCA which was fine if one was in a division where things were moving slowly as they were in the RCA Tube Division. But semiconductor companies like Texas Instruments and Intel were being run by young men who had no previous corporate training and they were leaving older companies like RCA and GE in their dust. When I argued that RCA had to modify it's approach to emulate these new companies, Lloyd saw that it was not politically feasible and he fired me. As it turned out, of course, I was right and RCA made a valiant attempt about two years later to follow my advice and actually fired Lloyd. However, it was too late and RCA never made it in semiconductors and integrated circuits.

Fortunately for me I still had friends at the RCA Laboratories and the head of the Labs at that time, Jim Hillier, offered me a job and I took it and never looked back. For the next 20 years I worked on a number of very interesting projects at the Labs, not as a researcher as such but as a manager of researchers. It was a wonderful time for me and I finally retired in 1986 as Staff Vice President of solid state research, a position that reported to the head of the Lab. I would say that my major achievement during that time was the part I played in negotiating a joint venture with Sharp Corporation in Japan. It was clear that such a joint venture was necessary if RCA was to remain in the integrated circuit business and we successfully made such a deal with Sharp, part of which was to build a $200 million facility in Washington state to engineer and manufacture chips. Alas, in 1985 GE bought RCA and the deal with Sharp never went through. I decided to retire and was asked to stay on 'till October 1986 to help with the "transition" which meant the total destruction of RCA as a corporation by GE. In the end, GE kept only NBC and sold off all the rest of the company piece by piece. The Laboratories became a part of Stanford Research Institute and my only association from that point on was as a consultant, a job which paid ridiculously well but which had no real interest for me.

In retrospect, I realize that I lived at a time when one could have a very rewarding career with a single company for 35 years and retire with a good pension. Those days are gone forever and I feel sorry for young people today who will never be able to experience that kind of a career.

MUSIC

I have already recounted my first attempt at learning a musical instrument which was the piano. Sometime around the time I was 9 or 10 I started to learn to play the trumpet. I'm not sure why I picked this instrument but it turned out to be a fortuitous choice. While I struck out miserably on the piano it turned out that I had a natural talent for playing the trumpet. I took lessons from a man by the name of Charles Andrews who was a wonderful cornet player and taught in the school system in Westfield, N.J., a town right next to Cranford where my family lived. Mr. Andrews started me on Arban's Trumpet Method which was the gold standard for trumpet methods in those days and still is. I also took lessons with Mr. Herman Royer who was a retired trumpet player and had played with a number of well known orchestras in New York City. When I was about 12 I formed a band with some grandchildren of Mr. Royer and a few other guys and we named ourselves "The Royal Sophisticates". We played "stock" arrangements which were available for 75 cents in those days and were used by all bands who couldn't afford to hire their own arranger. I also began my own arranging career with this band, a version of Glen Miller's "In The Mood" because the Miller arrangement was too difficult for our modest talents. We must have been pretty bad because, according to my mother, when we rehearsed at our house our dog, Tiny, would run upstairs and hide under the bed.

However, when I was about 14 we must have improved because we got a job playing for a New Years Eve party at a well known Cranford landmark called "The Casino". It was my first ever paying musical job for which I made $3, but it was a start. I played with this band until I was a Sophomore in high school and then I got a lucky break. There was a very good local band by the name of "The Ambassadors" and their lead trumpeter, a fellow named Carl Grozan, had the absolute lowest number in the military draft so they were without a trumpeter. I auditioned and got the job. "The Ambassadors" was the best band I ever played with. There were 3 sax's, 2 trumpets, a trombone and a rhythm section. We rehearsed once a week and usually had 1 job a week. It was tough going for me at first. It seemed like every 2 minutes the leader and lead sax player would stop the band and point out something that I had done wrong. But I learned more about how to play musically with this band than any other I ever played with. And we were good! We played all over NJ and even in New York City. But eventually the draft got too many members and the band broke up. But by that time I had another really great job after my Junior year in high school.

It was at the Hotel Wright in Asbury Park, N.J. and it was a dream job. There were 4 of us during the week and 5 on weekends. We played for dinner from 6:00 P.M. to 9:00 P.M. and then on Saturday we played at another hotel from 10:00 P.M. until 1:00 A.M. During the week I played bass and on the weekends I played trumpet. The guitar player was a real musical genius named Harold Chilton and he and I spent a lot of time when we were not at the beach writing arrangements where we treated the guitar as a horn, an idea which was new in those days. For this job we were paid $10 per week plus room and board and I must say that it was a fun experience all the way. We had all our days free and worked only 3 hours a night except on Saturday for which we received another $5.

The summer after I graduated from high school I got a job playing 7 nights a week at a night club on route 22 in Dunellen, N.J. The name of the club was "Princess Wana's" and it was indeed run by a woman called "Princess Wana". The Princess was supposedly a princess from a Native American tribe and she certainly looked the part. She ran the place, was there every night to welcome the guests and introduce the floor shows and take care of the band which meant free drinks and a midnight snack. The Princess was married to a guy named Mickey who had Mafia connections and if he had of been born 40 years later could have starred on "The Sopranos". The Princess was a wonderful boss and treated the members of our band very well indeed. Mickey, on the other hand, tolerated us as a necessary expense and the best we ever got from him was a curt nod when he arrived. There were four of us in the band. I played trumpet, Pete Billias played tenor sax and Vince Sabio was the leader and played piano. I don't remember the drummer's name. Our hours were from 9:00 P.M. until 2:00 A.M. We played 2 floor shows; one at 11 and one at 1. At twelve we received the aforementioned snack. For this I was paid $28 per week and I must say that I have never enjoyed any job more than the one at "Princess Wana's". There were many "characters" there, both in the floor shows and as customers. A regular customer was a girl named Kiki Roberts who had been a Zigfield Girl and was once the girl friend of a notorious gangster by the name of Legs Diamond. Legs had been ambushed by the FBI a number of years before in a telephone booth in New York. According to, Kiki, he had 72 bullets in him when they carried him out of the booth.

Kiki was not a big fan of the FBI and related this story to whomever would listen. One of the floor show dancers was a girl named Patsy. She did an "exotic" dance with a glass of water balanced on her forehead. Patsy was a rather heavy drinker but I saw her do this dance 84 times and she never spilled a drop! Another show stopper was a young couple from Haiti who did a dance with live fire torches. It was unbelievable that they could do this dance without being seriously burned, but in fact, they did, although they had a number of nasty scars from the years doing it. From my own perspective the most interesting person I met there was a girl named Toni. I kept a toy whistle on my music stand which I used in some novelty numbers and one night Toni walked up and took my whistle. When I went to reclaim it during intermission she said she would give it back to me if I would take her out. No girl had ever shown the slightest interest in me up to that point and I was so flabbergasted that I asked Pete what I should do. Pete said for me to take her out and since I had no car we decided on a double date; Pete with his girlfriend and me with Toni. Toni was short, dark and had a nice slim figure, a type that I have fallen for ever since. We started the date with dinner and then on the way home Toni and I were in the back seat of Pete's car when Toni kissed me. I'll never forget what she said next: "You're the worst kisser I ever met!". Then she said "Let me teach you." And she did. Although I have kissed a number of girls since, none of them could kiss like Toni. Not especially sexy but so warm and soft that I remember her to this day. I dated her a couple of more times but then after 6 weeks at "Princess Wana's" I had to leave for college and then the army and I never saw her again.

I never got my whistle back.

Music, and particularly playing the trumpet, has had a major impact on the kind of life that I have led. When I entered high school in 1939 I was a potential basket case if there ever was one. I was short, wore glasses, had acne, was poor at sports and was at best a "B" student. But after a month I realized that I could play the trumpet better than anybody else in the school, including seniors. From that moment on my high school career changed and soon everybody in the school knew that I was the best trumpet player. Once this was established I was allowed to participate in other school activities as well. In those days upon graduation it was the custom to sign everybody's year book and every person that signed mine had some positive comment about my trumpet playing. So it just proves that if one can do one thing better than anybody else his life is certainly made a lot easier.

After my job at "Princess Wana's" I attended Norwich University in Vermont. This was my father's decision and he made it because I wanted to continue playing trumpet as a career but he didn't believe that that was an appropriate career for me and in those days one did what their parents told them to do. Norwich was a military school and, as is usual for schools of this type, freshmen, called "rooks" at Norwich, were subject to incessant hazing. I took my share of this but when the upper class men found out that I was a really good trumpet player my burden was lifted to a great extent. Norwich had a dance band by the name of "The Grenadiers" and I was immediately promoted to play first trumpet with this band. The band was not up to the standards of "The Ambassadors" but it was not bad and we played all over the state of Vermont for other colleges and various other affairs.

After one semester at Norwich I volunteered (something that probably seems incredible to young men today but that's the way it was then) to serve in World War Two and was inducted into the army in February of 1943. I was assigned temporarily to Fort Devons in Massachusetts. I was appointed the official bugler and if they hadn't decided to use a recording somewhat later I would have probably spent the entire war there. I played trumpet for a number of other military musical organizations but it was not a major factor in my rather undistinguished military career. It did, however, result in me meeting a very beautiful Chinese girl when playing with a Filipino band in Shanghai after the war ended but more about her later.

After the war I returned to Norwich as a newly married man. I played throughout my remaining 3 years there and actually made more money playing the trumpet than I received from the GI Bill. Upon graduating from Norwich I attended graduate school at North Carolina State University where I was granted a teaching assistantship at $1200 per year. I stopped playing trumpet then and didn't take it up again for 12 years.

I really hadn't expected that I would ever play trumpet again but in 1961 a friend of mine at RCA told me that there was a group producing Gilbert and Sullivan operettas at McCarter Theater in Princeton and that they needed a trumpet player. I was dubious, but figuring that I had nothing to lose, I oiled up my Harry Glantz Conn and auditioned and got the job. Until then I had never played any type of classical music and it came as a shock to me that to play classical music on trumpet one had to learn to transpose. This means that you don't necessarily play the note that is written on the music but must transpose it to some other note according the a separate notation in the music.

After the Gilbert and Sullivan job I realized that if I was to make it as a classical trumpeter I had a lot of work to do. I took some lessons from two of the finest trumpet players in the New York area who happened to be teaching at Princeton at the time. One was John Ware who was assistant principal with the New York Philharmonic and the other was Ted Weiss who was principal with the New York City Ballet. Both these gentlemen were wonderful players and teachers and I learned a lot from them. They were also great actors in that they pretended that I could actually become a really good trumpeter when, of course, I knew better. I studied transposition, bought a C, D, and piccolo trumpet and began to get a lot of trumpet jobs with various organizations in this area. Two things helped me: first, there weren't a lot of good trumpet payers in the Princeton area at that time, and, second, Princess Diana had a trumpeter play the Purcell Trumpet Voluntary at her wedding. This resulted in every young bride wanting this music at her wedding and I got about 75 jobs playing this piece at weddings. I also played in many Messiahs at Christmas time and many other classical pieces. Four sopranos hired me to play the Bach Cantata Number 51 which is one of the more difficult pieces in the trumpet repertoire and somehow I managed to soldier through them all without total disaster. My classical trumpet playing ended about ten years ago when I played my last job on Easter 1999.

While all this was going on I also got connected with a quartet called Charlie Covert's Big Little band. I got into this band in the strangest of ways. First, the bass player got sick and I substituted for him. Then the piano player got sick and I substituted for him. Finally the trumpet player got sick and I substituted for him and when he didn't get well I became a permanent member of the band. I was the youngest member of the band and am the only survivor today. The band catered to older people and we got a lot of work playing the old standards, line dances and polkas. It was not really a very good band but all the guys were great and I enjoyed all the jobs I had with them.

Back when I was playing the summer job in Asbury Park, the bass player, Wally Roberts, taught me how to play piano by ear. So at the same time that I was playing all those trumpet jobs I also got a lot of work playing what some people call "Cocktail" piano. These were usually at private parties or at restaurants and though they were mostly boring every once in a while I got one with a bass player and drummer and those I really enjoyed.

When I retired from RCA in 1986 I started my recording studio. This was made possible by an innovation called MIDI which allowed one to arrange music, store it in a computer and then play it back with an orchestra consisting of electronic instruments. I have made about 35 CD's since then, about half with girl singers, and about half with just instruments, The only live parts are the vocals, the piano parts and the trumpet parts. None of these CD's have had the slightest commercial success but they have given me many hours of pleasure and I am still at it today, trying to fool my daughter into believing that she is hearing real musicians. Certainly music has been the most significant factor in my life and I am very grateful that I have had so much fun with a rather modest talent.

SOLDIER SAILOR

I volunteered to serve in the armed forces in the fall of 1942 but I was not inducted until February of 1943. After my brief service as bugler at Fort Devons I was sent to Atlantic City, New Jersey for basic training. I was quartered on the 12th floor of the Claridge Hotel which was, in peacetime, a luxurious place indeed. But for war service all the luxury had been removed. There were 4 of us in what had been a single room. It consisted of 2 up/down bunks and little else. Even the carpeting had been removed and all that was left was the concrete floor. The elevators had been retired and we walked up the 12 floors what seemed like a million times a day. However, all in all I had a relatively easy time in Atlantic City. Because of my military training at Norwich I was soon promoted to the position of drill master, which wasn't a real rank but which allowed me to waste endless days teaching recruits how to march in close order drill. I was in charge of perhaps 30 soldiers and we were the best marching group at the Claridge, largely because of what I had learned at Norwich. We marched with old Springfield rifles and I must say we were rather snappy indeed.

My only mishap in basic was when we were told to enter a tent with gas masks at our side and to wait until chlorine gas was introduced into the tent and then to put on our masks. My mask was defective and I signaled the officer in charge and he let me escape from the tent before any damage had been done. They gave me a new mask and I had to go through the whole procedure again without any problem.

I was then sent to Iowa City, Iowa to study at the University of Iowa to become a weather officer. At Iowa I met my first wife, Ethel, but other than that my stay there was uneventful. As was usual for the army, there had been a miscalculation as to how many weather officers they really needed and after six months our program was canceled and I found myself at Chanute Field in Illinois being trained, not as an officer, but as an enlisted man weather observer. Although I was disappointed it turned out that the training I received at Chanute was really excellent because I was picked to be in the equipment maintenance program so in addition to learning about taking weather measurements and plotting weather maps I also learned how to maintain internal combustion engines and electronic gear, mostly radios. After completing this course I was sent to Scott Field, Illinois as a member of the staff there where I worked an 8 hour shift as a weather man. It was easy work and I enjoyed it but I wanted to get over seas so I volunteered for a program called Spherics. This was a scheme to locate weather fronts with just three stations located at the points of a triangle about 700 miles from each other. I was assigned to China where Spherics was important because the weather in Japan follows the weather in China and with our 3 Spherics stations we could cover an area that would otherwise require perhaps 15 or so regular weather stations. I ended up at a small base (about 100 men including the 12 in our Spherics unit) just outside Sian, China. Sian was a wonderful city of about 500,000 people which existed as a self contained unit. All produce and meat were grown at farms outside the city and all manufacturing was done by artisans in the city itself. The city was surrounded by a huge wall and every night at midnight all doors to the city were sealed and no one entered or left until the next morning.

My time serving at Sian was without stress. The Japanese made a few feeble attempts to unload a bomb or two on us but their heart wasn't really in it. Then our base got a squadron of P-51's, probably the hottest fighter in WWII, and when they tried again and were all shot down by the P-51's they basically called it a day.

I had other adventures however. There was no opportunity to meet girls in Sian but there was a first class brothel and, like all my buddies, I visited there a few times. The protocol was fairly strict. One was expected to arrive around 6 in the evening, have dinner with the girls and spend the night. Once one had spent the night with a girl one was expected to choose her from then on. My girl was named Moo Soo and I must say in all honesty that I really didn't enjoy the time I spent with her, although it wasn't her fault. There just wasn't any chemistry there. On the other hand, my pal Jim McElroy (more about him later) had a partner who everybody called "School Girl" because she studied so hard to learn English and wanted to know everything there was to know about the U.S. One day Jim had the idea that we should take School Girl and Moo Soo to a spa about 35 miles away from Sian. We commandeered a Jeep and took off. After about 10 miles we noticed a group of about 8 guys on horses trailing us and the girls warned us that they were bandits. Jim was driving so it befell me to defend us. I took out my trusty carbine and let go about a dozen shots aimed roughly at our pursuers and that was the end of that. It's amazing what a little firepower can do in a situation like that.

There were almost no Caucasians in Sian but there was one Russian who made vodka and sold it to us for $1 a quart. But before we could buy any, he insisted that we visit his distillery where he proudly showed off his equipment and made every effort to prove that he made the best vodka this side of Moscow, and he was right, it was good. Another character was a Catholic priest from Italy who had lost all of his funding from Rome because of the war. His name was Father Baldoni and he was more or less adopted by our little Spherics group. We stole food from the mess hall and gave it to him to help feed his flock and in return he supplied us with red wine which I guess had originally been made for communion. Some GI's had fashioned a motor scooter out of spare parts and Father Baldoni used to drive it when he visited us, his black robes flowing out behind him with a surplus airplane wing tank full of red wine attached to the scooter's back. A memorable character if there ever was one!

When the war ended my pal McElroy, who was a real daredevil, talked me into sky-hiking into Shanghai which was strictly against regulations and if we had been caught would have resulted in serious consequences. But Jim could talk me into anything and we caught a ride to Shanghai on a C-47 that was delivering supplies to the new U.S. troops there. Except that there weren't any U.S. troops there and when we arrived we were surrounded by about a million Japanese soldiers. However, the Emperor had told them that the war was over and we were treated like visiting royalty. We stayed a couple of days, and then figuring that we had pushed out luck about as far as it was going to go, we caught another C-47 back to Sian.

About 3 weeks after Jim and I returned to Sian we were officially transferred to Shanghai to await a troop ship that would take us home. I don't remember how it happened but somehow I got a job playing trumpet with a Filipino band at a night club in Shanghai. There were 2 GI's in the band, the bass player and me. The Filipinos had been cut off from American music for 9 years and they were happy to have us teach them the latest songs from the States. It was on this job that I met a Chinese girl named Ling. I know that I have previously mentioned Ling as beautiful but that was true only of her personality. In fact she was rather plain looking but she was short, dark and had a slim almost boyish figure. We became friends and then lovers in a few days. I had had almost no experience with women at that time and it was difficult for me to believe that any girl liked to make love as much as I did. Ling was a very passionate and warm lover and she was also a drug addict. Her drug of choice was opium and we spent our nights in an "opium den" which was about the most peaceful place I have ever been in. Except for the bunk we shared everybody else in the place was totally stoned and as quiet as mice. Because of my totally square upbringing I never had the nerve to try a pipe but Ling smoked it every night and it seemed to make her even more warm and passionate than ever. I wish that this story ended in some kind of Madame Butterfly tragedy but that's not what happened. After about 3 weeks we had some kind of stupid spat which was entirely my uptight American fault and I told her that I never wanted to see her again. She had never asked me for money so it was probably some kind of stupid jealousy thing on my part. Ling was a tough cookie but when I told that we were finished I saw the semblance of a tear in her eye. Of course, after a few days I realized what a total jerk I had been and I spent many hours trying to find her. But she had literally disappeared and I never saw her again. Our relationship was doomed from the beginning and we both knew that but I wish to this day, 65 years later, that I had behaved decently to a very sweet and wonderful girl.

Around January 1, 1946 I boarded the General Eltinge troop ship for the journey home and it was one of the worst experiences of my life. When I was going overseas we always flew and so this was my first time on a troop ship. For 23 days I spent most of my time in the lowest bunk in D deck which was the lowest level in the ship, just above the bilge. The food was terrible, there were no stairs (only ladders) and when we were allowed up on deck we were subjected to the sights of officers and nurses frolicking on the deck above us. However, I finally got home and was discharged from the Army in March of 1946.

While in the Army I had many friends for which there has never been a counterpart in civilian life. I guess the reason is that when one is in the army one spends 24 hours a day with one's fellow soldiers, you eat with them, sleep in the same barracks or tent with them and spend any leisure time you have with them. There is no equivalent relationship in civilian life and although one's army friendships last only a year or so they persist in your memory until you die. I had a number of such friendships:

Charlie Rossi. I met Charlie when I was in basic training in Atlantic City. He was about 25 years old at that time and was divorced. Charlie was not well educated but he was a deep thinker and a philosopher. Since there was nothing else to do in Atlantic City we spent almost all of our liberty talking and drinking. Charlie taught me to drink Boilermakers, which consist of a glass of beer with a shot glass of booze dropped in it. I never saw Charlie again after basic but I remember him to this day.

Don Adkins. Don was a Jew from Chicago who was legally blind. He wore Coke bottle glasses and cheated on his eye exam so that he could get into the army. He was my first friend who was really a liberal and many of the ideas that he exposed me to persist in my attitudes today. Don was also an excellent alto sax player and we played together in a band that was formed when I was in Iowa City.

Jerry Stryker. Jerry was a Jew from New York and was quite a few years older than the rest of us in Sian. Jerry was very smart and in addition was a truly wonderful magician. All of Jerry's tricks were done without props of any kind. He could manipulate coins and cards with truly amazing dexterity. I have seen Jerry take a deck of cards shuffled by another person and deal himself 4 aces just like that. For that reason Jerry refused to play cards with anybody if money was involved.

Al Ham. Al was with me in Iowa City and was the spark plug behind forming our band there. He had been the bassist with the Artie Shaw Orchestra and was an excellent musician. He took a group of players who were about 5 notches down from where he was and turned us into a fairly decent group.

Murray Fisher. I met Murray on the trip home on the General Eltinge. Murray was the funniest guy I ever met and his constant jokes and good humor almost made the trip acceptable. Murray never let on that his family was very wealthy and I only found this out when sometime after the war he invited a few of us to lunch at his parents apartment over looking Central Park. It was the only true mansion that I have ever been in. There was a butler, 2 maids, a cook etc. but Murray was as funny as ever and we had a great time.

Jim McElroy. Jim was probably the best friend I have ever had although he was also probably the worst influence. He cared nothing for authority and flouted it with impunity. Somehow he avoided getting court marshaled but he came close. Since I was a nerd we formed an unlikely pair. Jim had talked me into a number of hairy experiences, some of which I have already related. When the war ended he insisted that we should go to South America as soldiers of fortune. He thought we could have many adventures there and make a lot of money too. Of course this was impossible for me to agree to and although he persisted right up to the day we separated in Seattle I just didn't have the right personality to do it. As a result he became so pissed off at me that I never heard from him again. I often wonder if he did, in fact go, and if so what happened to him.

There were many others but these are the ones that persist in my memory most vividly after 65 years.

In summary, the 37 months I spent in the army were not all fun by any means but I came home with all my limbs and with enough experiences to last a lifetime. All in all I'm happy that I had the chance.

In September of 1946 I returned to Norwich to complete my college education as a beneficiary of the GI Bill. As a result of my 37 months in the army as an enlisted man I had decided that if there were any more wars I was going to participate as a commissioned officer. During the war I had had my share of disputes with officers and, of course, I lost them all. Even today, the military treats officers completely different than they treat enlisted personnel. During my senior year at Norwich I applied for and was granted a commission as an Ensign in the United States Navy Reserve. To maintain one's commission, all one had to do was take correspondence courses supplied by the

Navy by mail and show up for 2 weeks of active duty once a year. I was assigned to that part of the Navy responsible for breaking codes and ciphers. It was interesting work. The courses started way back with the so-called Caesar cipher and continued up to the types of ciphers used in 1949. Compared to today's computer ciphers they were primitive indeed but at the time I enjoyed learning about them. Twice I went on active duty for 2 weeks, once in Washington, D.C. and once in Charleston S.C. I bought a snazzy tan officer's uniform and with my 2 little gold bars I played at being an officer in the U.S Navy. I even got promoted to LTJG. Of course it was a farce. I had never served on a ship and didn't know the bow from the stern but it was fun. I wish now that I had continued in the program because after 20 years I would be entitled to a Navy pension. But I dropped out after about 3 years, one of the many dumb things that I have done over the years.

SCHOOL

My early school days were so uneventful that I have no real memories of them. I guess I was an average student. My first real recollection of school was when I entered High School. If it hadn't been for my trumpet playing these 4 years would have probably been a total disaster. I did manage to graduate in 1942 and what followed was my job at Princess Wana's and my attendance at Norwich University. My prewar Norwich time was uneventful also except for my trumpet playing there in The Grenadiers.

After the war Norwich had a policy that if one was a veteran of WWII, had attended Norwich before the war and was married one was exempt from any further military activity in the Corps of Cadets. About 40 of us qualified for this exemption and we constituted a subgroup of students outside of the normal Norwich student body. We were housed in a small cluster of prefabricated houses off-campus and our only obligation was to show up for classes. My wife, Ethel, and I occupied one half of one of these houses. We had a living room, a bedroom, a kitchen and a bath. The only heat was a large kerosene unit in the living room and all the cooking was done on a kerosene stove. Our ice box was the kind that one actually had to put ice in. It was primitive but to us it was like a mansion. Everybody else lived in identical houses and we formed a fairly close-knit little community.

After 3 years in the army I found the academic work at Norwich to be relatively easy and, unlike my High School days, I got very good grades. I finished 2nd in my class of about 75. I still remember the guy who beat me whose name was Oakley Davis.

I decided that it would be a good idea to attend graduate school so I applied to about 4 or 5 and I was accepted by all of them but chose North Carolina State because they offered me the best assistantship, i.e., $1,200 per year to teach half time and attend classes half time. Between this and the GI Bill we managed to get along for 2 years. We lived in a very small apartment that had once been a garage and we were lucky to get that. The head of the EE Department, Dr. Brenecke found it for us and he took an interest in my work at NC State for the whole time I was there. Most of the classes I taught were to non-EE students who were required to take one course in Electrical Engineering. Of course, the majority of these students had no interest whatsoever in electricity and it was quite a challenge to keep them awake for 50 minutes. However I was awarded the singular honor of teaching EE seniors a course in Fields which had previously been taught by Dr. Brenecke himself.

Unlike Norwich, the work at N.C. State was hard and I had to put in a lot of effort to do well. I did manage to graduate with a Master's Degree in 1951 and this time I was first in my class of about 20 students.

Near the end of my second year I attended a presentation by a representative from RCA Laboratories and as a result of attending this presentation I applied for and got the job there. I almost didn't go to that presentation and have often wondered how different my life would have been if I had missed it.

I would be remiss if I didn't comment on what it's like to live in the South in 1949. We arrived in Raleigh on a Saturday afternoon and decided to stay at a rooming house on Hillsboro Avenue, the main drag in Raleigh. Our landlady welcomed us and asked us 3 questions: our name, where we were from and where we would be attending church the next morning.

My wife had been raised as a Lutheran but our landlady didn't know of any Lutheran churches so she suggested that we attend her church, which was Presbyterian. So, believe it or not, we attended church every Sunday for the next 2 years. We met a lot of very nice people at that church. The were very friendly, invited us to their homes for dinner and made sure we were welcomed to all kind of church socials. But after about 3 months we began to notice things that made us feel uncomfortable. There were endless signs saying "White" and "Colored", we noticed that black people always went to the back of the bus even if there were plenty of seats up front and there very few black people on the streets in downtown Raleigh and if you met one they would defer to you and move off the sidewalk. After about 6 months we began to get advice from our Southern friends which went something like this: "You Yankees don't know how to treat your Nigras (I never heard them use the term "nigger" or black, it was always Nigra). We treat them all right but every once in a while we have to string one of them up so the rest of them realize how good they have it here". They were especially fearful of school integration. Their fear was that if the races were allowed to mix then some big black Nigra would seduce their little virgin girls and this would lead to a population of people with polluted Nigra blood. Of course, this was long before such examples of this polluted blood like Barrack Obama, Derek Jeeter and Tiger Woods were born. Although we didn't treat black people in New Jersey all that much better than they did, I was still appalled at their racism. I was used to black kids in the Cranford schools and found it hard to believe that they could get so upset about nothing. But I kept my mouth shut and we left North Carolina 2 years later without incident.

RELATIONSHIPS

Except for my army days, the only important relationships I have had have been with women. As I have previously mentioned all my important relationships with men occurred when I was in the military even though they lasted for only a year or 2. I have been blessed, or cursed, with no sexual interest in men which is probably the only way for a man to have an important relationship with another man in civilian life. There may be a few other exceptions like being in the Mafia. Although I have known many men whom I guess I would call friends, none of them have affected my life in any really important way.

When I was 17 and a senior in high school I caught what was probably the definitive condition of "Puppy Love". The object of my adoration was a 14 year old sophomore by the name of Ruth Parsons. Like almost all the girls I have fallen for since, Ruth was short, dark and slim. But the principal reason I fell for her was that she was an excellent violinist. We originally became acquainted when we were both performing in a production of Gilbert and Sullivan's "The Mikado". Our love affair was intense, at least on my side, but chaste. The nearest we ever came to physical love was one night when I took her canoeing on the Raritan river, which ran through Cranford. My father had given me a Zenith portable radio and I must say it was a rather romantic sight as we paddled down the river with the Zenith blaring out Glenn Miller. However, it turned out that Ruth was nowhere near as enamored with me as I was with her and she soon dumped me and took up with one of my best friends, Bob Livingston.

I met my first wife, Ethel Carpenter, when I was stationed in Iowa City in 1943. I don't remember how we met but it was probably at some kind of USO dance. Ethel was a very quiet and bashful girl and as I got to know her I began to think that maybe we could have a romance and fall in love. Ethel was an orphan and was raised by a lady in Iowa City but I don't remember how or why they ended up together. By the time I left Iowa City we had made plans that after the war we would get married. Unlike most encounters of this kind, we, in fact did get married on February 9, 1946. About a year before I was discharged from the army Ethel moved to Cranford in order to live with my mother and father. My mother was originally opposed to our getting married but my father fell in love with Ethel from the start. Once we were married my mother also came to love her and there was never a problem with their relationship after that. One event impressed my father enormously. Ethel had gotten a job in New York but one morning she had been let go. Rather than come home, she applied for and got another job the same day, a job she held until we got married. She also worked the 5 years it took me to get through college and graduate school. One of her bosses in Vermont for whom she worked the 3 years we were there kept in touch with her for 30 years after we left Vermont. When we left North Carolina in 1951 she was pregnant with our daughter, Kristine, and from that time on she made a beautiful home for Kristine and me and did a lot of volunteer work. Ethel had a green thumb and could probably have raised roses in the Sahara Desert. She also was an excellent interior decorator and cook.

Like all marriages, ours had its ups and downs but I can honestly say that 90% of the downs were my fault. We were married 54 years before she was taken from this life by Alzheimer's Disease.

PUBLISHED
LETTERS TO THE
EDITOR

To The Editor:

I think it's terrible what liberals have done to this country.

If it weren't for liberals:

Politicians wouldn't have to waste a lot of time and money trying to get the women's vote and the black vote because there wouldn't be any women's vote or black vote.

The solvency of Social Security and Medicare wouldn't be a problem because there wouldn't be any Social Security or Medicare.

The immigration problem wouldn't have arisen because employers would still be able to hire 10-year-old kids for 15 cents an hour and there would be no incentive for Mexican illegal aliens to come here.

Gay marriage wouldn't be a problem because all the homosexuals would be in jail.

And if it weren't for today's crybaby liberals constantly yapping about global warming, civil liberties, health care, income inequity, the war, etc., we could forget about those items as well.

It just makes my blood boil when I think of the paradise on earth this country would be if it weren't for those darn liberals!

Robert D. Lohman
Trenton Times 3/10/2008

To The Editor:

The recent attacks by a Republican ex-congressman and fellow presidential candidate on Mitt Romney for making a lot of money and paying relatively small taxes is like a circus turned upside-down.

Mr. Romney didn't enact the laws that enabled him to amass a fortune and keep most of it-Congress did!

And the vast majority of Republicans embrace those laws enthusiastically.

There may be other reasons to deny Mr. Romney the nomination, but making a lot of money and paying 15 percent in taxes is not among them.

Robert Lohman
Trenton Times 2/12/2012

To The Editor:

Here's an idea. Why not give all the recipients of Medicare a choice?

Keep your Medicare as it now is, or opt out of Medicare and join a private insurance plan.

Since about half of Medicare recipients are Republicans, they would opt out. This would accomplish two things:

1) It would reduce the cost of Medicare by a factor of two.
2) It would allow these Republicans to get out from under the terrible yoke of "socialized medicine" which they have borne so bravely ever since they were 65.

Would it happen? Sure, when pigs fly.

Robert D. Lohman
Trenton Times 8/21/2009

To The Editor:

I don't know whether former Republican presidential candidate Herman Cain, who has suspended his campaign amid allegations of sexual harassment and illicit affairs, would make a good or bad president, but I think he is taking a bad rap for his romantic foibles.

JFK, LBJ and Bill Clinton are among our most notable and respected presidents and all three were world-class Casanovas. If the Republicans really want to reduce the size of the federal government, all they have to do is insist that every member of Congress and the executive branch who has had an extramarital affair resign.

I don't know if we can run the country with three people, but it might be fun to try.

Robert D. Lohman
Trenton Times 12/6/2011